ON TEMPESTUOUS SEAS

By the same author:

Ar Fôr Tymhestlog

On Tempestuous Seas
Rowing Two Oceans

Elin Haf Davies

First published in 2011

© Elin Haf Davies

© Gwasg Carreg Gwalch 2011

Published with the financial suport
of the Welsh Books Council

ISBN: 978-1-84527-360-6

Cover design: Welsh Books Council

Published by Gwasg Carreg Gwalch,
12 Iard yr Orsaf, Llanrwst, Wales LL26 0EH
tel: 01492 642031
fax: 01492 641502
email: books@carreg-gwalch.com
website: www.carreg-gwalch.com

Dedication

To my parents,
for the never-ending love and support that you've given me.

To my nephews and nieces,
Ilan Aled, Dafydd Robert, Heledd Wyn, Non Wyn,
Gwion Tomos, Sara Fflur, Sion Gwilym and Catrin Ann,
my godson Rhun Llwyd, and his brother Ynyr Llwyd:
may you live your dreams –
whatever they may be.

And to all that made my two crossings possible.
I can't name you all, but a special 'thank you' must go to
Jamie Hopkins, Lucy Jameson, Jo Bardoe, Mike Baker,
Frank and Ollie Garrigue –
not forgetting, of course, Herdip Sidhu, Sarah Duff,
Fiona Waller and Jo Jackson
for not throwing me overboard!

Prologue

There is no living thing that is not afraid when it faces danger.
The true courage is in facing danger when you are afraid.

L. Frank Baum
The Wonderful Wizard of Oz

In the timeless film classic *The Wizard of Oz* a team of three characters, seemingly insufficient in their own minds to achieve their goal of helping a little girl get back home, fearfully petitioned the Great Oz. When the Wizard was revealed, he granted their requests by bestowing upon them symbolic gifts reflecting three of the greatest attributes necessary in conquering any great challenge – intellect, courage, and heart. Of these, heart is perhaps the greatest. In granting the Tin Man's request, the Wizard presented him with a heart on a chain that contained within it a clock. From this example, three things are readily apparent: first, to have heart requires an abiding sense of purpose and passion to be firmly connected, chained if you will, to your very being; second, it symbolises feelings and emotions, both of which must be conjoined for courage to be expressed in its greatest dimension; and finally, the clock reminds us that the time for intellect, heart and courage during our human existence are often immediately apparent and also both finite and infinite in nature.

In all of human medicine, there is no greater intersection of fear and courage as when a revelation of a protracted, certain death is given to a patient – and in paediatrics in particular, to the parents of a child. In the summer of 2008, Craig and Charlotte Benson noticed that something was not right with their beautiful five-year-old daughter, Christiane. A complex medical evaluation revealed that Christiane suffered from neuronal ceroid lipofuscinoses - Batten's disease, a rare autosomal recessive genetic disease (2–4 cases per 100,000 live births) which has no treatment, involves progressive loss of vision, the onset of seizures, severe movement disorder, loss of cognitive function and culminates in death, usually before the second decade of life. Christiane would never drive a car, get a college education, attend her graduation or have the chance to be given away in marriage by her father. Another little girl, Mia, cared for at Great Ormond Street Hospital by a research nurse, Elin Haf Davies, faced a similar uncertain future and hopelessness that is associated with an inherited, rare disease. In the case of Christiane, her father became dedicated to the quest of engaging the best that science had to offer in order to diagnose, and hopefully one day produce, a treatment for Batten's disease. As for Mia, her inspirational challenge provided the fuel that would propel a farmer's daughter from north Wales into a great life adventure – rowing across the vast expanse of the Atlantic Ocean in The World's Toughest Rowing Race.

To love is to risk not being loved in return.
To hope is to risk pain.
To try is to risk failure, but risk must be taken,
Because the greatest hazard in life is to risk nothing.
Leo Buscaglia

Conquest is the opiate for the adventurer.
Gregory Kearns, 2011

Temporarily leaving loved ones, a profession, a successful career progression and one of the most important positions involved with the development of safe and effective drug treatments for children across Europe, to crawl, with a trusted colleague and friend, into a small wooden row boat headed for a 'holiday' in the Caribbean is something done only by a young woman that enjoys playing rugby! As I sat for dinner in Geneva with Elin Haf Davies following a World Health Organisation meeting and listened to this captivating plan, I could hardly believe what my ears were hearing. Whilst the words 'fear', 'courage', 'adventure', 'brilliance', 'devotion', 'amazement', 'stupidity' and 'challenge' flashed across the screen of my mind, this young woman articulated to me a detailed, grand plan for this adventure – and, moreover, a complete, logic- and purpose-driven perspective of why she MUST undertake it. At the end of dinner, it all made perfect sense, just as it did again almost a year after her becoming the first Welsh woman to row across the Atlantic.

This time, after my first adventure with black pudding and an afternoon of intense, analytical discussion prefaced as thinly veiled career consultation, Elin announced that she was going to do it all over again, but this time with three other women that she hardly knew, all of whom were purposed to win a rowing race across the Indian Ocean. Clearly, 'once' for Elin would, in life, never be enough and the euphoria and great relief that came with conquest became a propulsion system for character and an ever present need to perpetuate the doing of good.

My definition of courage is never letting anyone define you.
Jenna Jameson
Esquire magazine, 2008

A trip across two oceans in a row-boat would be seen by many as a defining life experience. However, when you finish the last page of this book, you will see that for its author, now Dr Davies, the adventure was far more than that. In the pages that follow, you will find a captivating description of not merely some amazing adventures, but rather, how the human spirit is engaged with others, within and with that which is beyond our control. It is not simply a profile in courage, but rather, a testimonial on the value of a purpose-driven existence in using the power and passion within oneself to create opportunity for others. Finally, the words between the covers of this book will teach you, as they have for me, many important lessons about life: namely, to be driven by a sense of purpose greater than yourself and to realise that your life will be enriched in measure by what you do because of and on behalf of others. The story of Elin's adventures will reveal that the true examples of resilience, determination and perseverance in overcoming the odds in life have little to do with what we do, but rather, why and how that we do it.

A true adventure in life never really ends.

Gregory L. Kearns, Pharm.D, PhD
The Children's Mercy Hospitals
Kansas City, Missouri, USA

Marion Merrell Dow/Missouri Chair of Medical Research
Professor of Pediatrics and Pharmacology, UMKC
Chairman, Department of Medical Research
Associate Chairman, Department of Pediatrics
Director, Pediatric Pharmacology Research Unit

1

Baptism of fire

Years from now you will be more disappointed
by the things you didn't do
than the ones you did do.

So throw off the bow lines.
Sail away from the safe harbour.
Catch the trade winds in your sails.
Explore. Dream. Discover.
Mark Twain

Call on God, but row away from the rocks.
Indian proverb

Wave after wave crashed towards us, the roaring noise engulfing me in fear. The all-consuming darkness meant that I couldn't see which direction the waves came from, and I'd be thrown off my seat unceremoniously whenever a rogue wave crashed into us. The clouds were so dark and low that the stars couldn't cast any of their light through. Oh why wasn't there a full moon with its light to help us on the start of our voyage? I cursed.

The dim light of El Hierro was still visible on the horizon, as a constant reminder of the land from which we were desperately trying to escape. I closed my eyes, in the hope that would improve the rest of my senses, and in a pathetic attempt to stop any more tears from rolling down my cheeks.

Another wave in the distance gathered pace before crashing over me and our small boat, *Dream Maker*. The Atlantic sea and my salty tears mixed into one. I shivered as the freezing cold water got inside my jacket, and ran down my neck. I could see Herdip, my team mate, lying in the cabin. Herdip, the only other member of the crew, my only company for the forthcoming days, weeks and months. Fulfilling a dream? This was going to be a nightmare.

Hardly eighteen hours had passed since we left the isle of La Gomera, with Mam, Dad and my sister Glesni waving us off. Leaving the three of them standing nervously on the harbour wall amongst dozens of other supporters, while I battled to be cheerful and excited about the adventure that lay ahead, determined not to show any emotion. I didn't want to appear to be weak. I had no idea what my parents were thinking as I rowed towards the horizon, slowly disappearing out of sight.

What emotions, I wondered, consumed their hearts? I could imagine. They probably had doubts whether they would ever see me again. This was a heart-rending experience. I longed to be back with them – now! If I hadn't been so frightened a few hours earlier I would have turned our boat back towards land, to be with them. But the fear of being cast upon the rocks of El Hierro now dictated my every action. In our current situation we were better off getting away from land, away from the rocks, and away from Mam, Dad and Gles, and rowing as hard and as fast as I could out into the vast unknown of the Atlantic Ocean.

Recent events played heavily on my mind. The fright of having the night's darkness replaced in an instant by piercing bright lights was nearly the end of me. It blinded me completely and I was convinced that a tanker ship had appeared from nowhere and was about to crash into us.

I dropped the oars in fright, and to protect my eyes from the bright light. Then a faceless voice shouted across the waves 'Dream Maker, Dream Maker, Dream Maker ... switch your VHF to channel sixteen'. I tripped over the oars as I clumsily stepped towards the cabin. 'Dream Maker, this is Zara,' announced the voice over the radio. 'We've been tracking your course. If you continue on this course you'll be taken north of the island, and disqualified from the race. You're also at risk of being washed against the rocks. You must change your bearing immediately! I repeat: you must change your bearing immediately! Over.'

Then silence. Complete silence. I was frozen with fear. In my mind a thousand questions raced. How? Where? When? Why? Why indeed? Why had I chosen to leave my friends and family and all of my home comforts, a couple of weeks before Christmas, to be in a 24-foot rowing boat, venturing across 2,500 miles of the Atlantic Ocean? Embarking on an unknown and uncomfortable experience. But I didn't have time then to contemplate those issues. At that second I had to concentrate on our current situation. Focus, and make a decision that would save us from the rocks and keep us in the race. With some additional words of advice from the experienced crew on Zara, and another examination of our charts, I set another bearing to aim for. Minutes later I was back on the oars, and Herdip was once more trying to catch some sleep. The bright light had long disappeared and the darkness of the night was once more pressing on me. The reality of our situation was finally sinking in, and an understanding of what we were trying to achieve dawned on me.

The Atlantic Ocean rowing race – The World's Toughest Rowing Race, according to Woodvale Challenge, the race organisers. And there I was, a farmer's daughter from north Wales with barely a day's experience of being out at sea, and with only a few hours' rowing lessons, as one of the competitors. This was insane. We hadn't seen any of the other competitors for hours by now, and wouldn't see any of them again while out at sea. This was a race against the clock, against the waves, and against whatever else the mighty ocean chose to throw at us.

My confidence was shattered. We didn't have the ability, the know-how or the experience to do this. The first few hours had already proved as much, as we had tracked the coastline rather than a compass bearing. What on earth made me think I could participate, let alone compete, in such a brutal challenge? We didn't even have the VHF radio on the right channel! Eighteen hours, a little over 20 nautical miles, and already the possibility of retiring from the race and abandoning our dream was becoming a real possibility. Two years of planning, £63,000 of costs and all just to give up in the first day. I couldn't give up now, could I? What about all the people who had supported us, taught us to row, generously giving of their time and money to help us prepare for the race? And what all about all the others who doubted our ability even to row out of the harbour? Was I about to disappoint so many people, and prove all the doubters right? I focused on the small light of the compass, and the bearing we were now taking. I started to sing to pass the time, to mute the noise of the waves and to boost my morale. Deep down I knew that things would get much harder than this, and I didn't want to give up on the first obstacle. Whatever would happen, I had a challenge to conquer, a dream to fulfil. I certainly wouldn't give up quite so soon.

At last day broke, and I could see a tiny speck of sunlight appearing on the horizon. A sign that we had conquered our first night out at sea – although it was a pretty bitter comfort knowing how many more days and nights we had ahead of us. I studied my watch. I'd been rowing for nearly two hours, so I called for Herdip, to warn her that it was nearly time to swap over. Slowly, Herdip made her way out of the cabin, putting her life jacket on and attaching the harness to her ankle. She said nothing. Seasickness had struck and she was clearly suffering badly. The look in her eyes betrayed both our feelings. I couldn't think of anything worthwhile to say, so I said nothing. I clambered into the cabin that suddenly appeared to be incredibly snug, despite how small it was. I attempted to get undressed while being thrown from one side of the cabin to the other. Finally I lay in the sleeping bag that was still warm from Herdip's body. I looked up on the cabin roof where we'd written motivational words to help keep us going through the difficult times. Amongst them there was a short prayer that Nain, my Gran, had given me before I left. I read it over and over again.

Ni fethodd gweddi daer erioed
A chyrraedd hyd y nen.
Ac mewn cyfyngder, Elin, rhed ar dy union ato Ef.

An earnest prayer never fails,
To reach our God above,
And in distress, Elin, run to Him directly.

I was praying that the shivering would stop and that Nain, in turn, had prayed for me before falling asleep last night. Nain could always put a smile on my face. Sleep was sure to improve spirits, and make the situation seem brighter ...

2

Back in the beginning

There are only two lasting bequests we can give our children.
One is roots, the other wings.
Hodding Carter

His world was Welsh, his Wales world wide.
Carwyn Rees James (1929-1983)

The moment that I decided to row across the Atlantic came shortly after leaving Steve, my husband. After a nine-year relationship, including nearly seven years of marriage, it was difficult to cope with the split, even though I was the one that bought the relationship to an end. But in hindsight, my desire to explore was probably there before I was ever married, just silenced briefly while I conformed to the social norm.

I was born in July 1976 – a hot summer by all accounts, and the inspiration for my second name, Haf (which means 'summer'). I was raised on Tŷ Cerrig farm in the small Welsh village of Parc and all my childhood memories are of sunshine and bright blue skies over the Arennig Fawr mountain. I'm the youngest daughter to Gwilym and Olwen, and a little sister to Dylan, Meilir and Glesni. My siblings are very close in age and some years older than me. Dylan and Meilir would often tease that I had been adopted from a broken family in Yorkshire. But as we grew it was easy to see that the family resemblance betrayed their story. Being the 'baby' of the family was very advantageous, while

I was a child – and beyond! I had endless care and attention from my parents, and much more freedom than the other three, according to them! Poor Glesni spent many an hour having to entertain me, and it is of little surprise that she pushed me off the swing and broke my arm once! My upbringing was happy and loving, and there was no reason for the constant interest in escaping to explore the world. But that was how I felt, and there was nothing I could do to escape those feelings.

There is no rational explanation of how a childhood in the Welsh mountains of Penllyn leads to the desire to be out on the immense ocean with all its dangers. It would make more sense for my rural upbringing to lead to the desire to climb Everest! As a child even the beauty of Llyn Tegid, the lake near Bala, hadn't been enough to persuade me to partake in water sports. The closest I'd been was sitting in a St John's Ambulance on the banks of Afon Tryweryn patching up any unfortunate canoeist who crashed against the rocks. But I have very vivid memories of wanting, at twelve years old, to cross the border to see the world, every corner of it.

I was educated at Parc primary school, amongst fifteen other pupils at most. I truly believe that being a pupil in such a small school gave me confidence and roots, and this has made embarking on adventures and challenges so much easier. After all, everything is easier when you have a safe anchor in place, wherever you may be in the world. Unfortunately, the future of Parc primary school looks uncertain as financial constraints and a few opinionated councillors campaign to close the school gates. Eight of the current nineteen pupils are my nieces and nephews, and as five generations of our family has started their educational life at that school the threat to us is a brutal one. If the school is ever forced to shut, the children of Parc will miss out on so much more than just a brilliant education. A secure home and a good education are the best roots that anyone could wish for – and my childhood in Parc gave me both.

Parc is almost totally Welsh-speaking and I spoke hardly any English until I was eight or nine years old. Community life in Parc is a rich tapestry of Welsh culture, where singing, drama group and a vibrant community spirit reigns. I firmly believe that it was the perfect place to be as a child.

Agriculture and religion were another two of the prominent features of community life as I grew up, and to some extent that remains true today. The minister in Parc at the time was the Reverend Bryn Ellis, brother to the famous Welsh-language author Islwyn Ffowc Ellis. I was christened, confirmed and married by Mr Ellis, and his influence upon us all as a family was immense. His son, Aled was also a close family friend, and for many years he worked with Dad on our farm. It was a tragic loss when Aled was killed in a car accident at twenty-seven years of age. The devastation was felt by his parents, friends and all the local community. I was only eleven years old at the time, and realised, for the first time, how fragile life was.

> *As is a tale, so is life: not how long it is,*
> *but how good it is, is what matters.*
> Seneca

The chapel in Parc was a prominent feature in my upbringing. Dad is a deacon there, and Taid, my grandfather, was also a deacon there for sixty-three years. Attending Sunday school and service was an unbroken ritual in our family life. My grandparents were both awarded the Medal Gee for their continued commitment to the Sunday school. Watching Taid kneel at the altar to recite *Gweddi'r Arglwydd* – the Lord's Prayer – made an impression on me even at a young age. My grandparent's faith was beyond anything I could comprehend, let alone follow.

I have countless memories of both sets of grandparents, Trebor and Megan, and Dei Morris and Mari. The four lived locally in Bala and played a big part in my childhood. I was extremely fortunate to be eighteen years old before the first sadly passed away. I'd frequently visit Trebor and Megan for tea after school, and chat away while teacakes were toasted on the open fire of the Aga. I would also frequently stay over with them on Saturday nights, and the Sunday ritual would always be the same – arriving at chapel some twenty minutes before the start of service.

Nain Mari, my Dad's mum, and I were particularly close friends, and we shared many secrets over the years. Sharing a secret with Nain was certainly safer than investing money in any bank. She was brilliant at expressing her view. She said it as she saw it, and her honesty was a breath of fresh air. She missed out on nothing, and she'd regularly ask 'Did you get a kiss on Saturday night?' She lived her life with a beaming smile, and I admired that greatly, along with the particularly lively and loving relationship she and Taid had, even after sixty-three years of marriage. It was a huge loss when Nain peacefully passed away at 101 years of age. Part of me had started to believe that Nain would live forever. Some people say that my personality is a mixture of Nain's and my Aunty Nia's, my Mam's sister. It's fair to admit that I'm as determined as both, a trait which I think has stood me in good stead.

My secondary education was at Ysgol y Berwyn in nearby Bala, where the years passed with a greater emphasis on socialising and volunteering for St John's Ambulance than on learning. Even so, I managed to pass all eleven of my GCSEs and left school (and home) to study for my A levels at Gwynedd Technical College in Bangor, fifty miles away from Parc. I wanted to study Human Biology, Psychology and Sociology in preparation for my nurse training and Ysgol y Berwyn didn't offer those subjects, so a move to Bangor was the obvious choice. The move was also the first time that I had to study in English rather than Welsh, and a practice run for my later move to London. My life in Bangor was again more focused on socialising rather than on learning, especially in my last year, after I secured a place to train as a children's nurse, regardless of my A level grades! Needless to say, my A level results were nothing to write home about!

At eighteen, after four years of dreaming, I flew out to Lesotho in South Africa to be a volunteer with the charity Save the Children. Since 1985 an independent charity named Dolen Cymru (meaning 'Wales Link') has been creating life-changing links between Wales and Lesotho, developing a crucial relationship in education, health, governance and civil society. The mountainous landscapes, and multi-lingual communities, mean that Wales and Lesotho have more in common than one would initially imagine. Through Dolen Cymru, I was then able to link up with Save the Children, and since I had known from a very young age that I wanted to work with children, it was an obvious and easy choice.

With the incredible support of the community in Parc I had worked hard to raise the money to allow me to be there, and I'd also succeeded in a much harder task – persuading my parents to let me go. Like all other parents, I'm sure they had reservations about my plans and felt that I was too young and too inexperienced to venture there to face many unknowns.

I volunteered in an orphanage around eight miles outside the capital city, Maseru. I lived in a round hut with a thatched roof, which was pure luxury compared to the children's living quarters. The children were shared between two dorms, one for the boys and one for the girls, despite the huge difference in age, and all of them sleeping on mattresses on the floor. It was all considerably different from Tŷ Cerrig. Part of my responsibility there as a volunteer was to wash and dress the children, help them with school work and generally entertain them. One of the most popular activities was to sing, dance and perform various plays – the favourite being 'Little Red Riding Hood'. In so many ways it felt just like community life in Parc. Only one of the children, Teboho, was able to speak English when I arrived, and he became a particularly close friend. Both of us spent many hours giving English lessons to the others, and I quietly hope now that one or two of them continue to speak English with a Welsh accent! Even though the children were all incredibly loving and lively, I still experienced extreme loneliness. I was missing my friends and family so much and a *hiraeth* (deep longing) for Wales tore through me. I frequently received letters and parcels from everyone at home, and I loved hearing all the news. It was also a brilliant treat to receive all the gifts – even if all the chocolate had melted to nothing after leaving the winter chill of Wales for a hot African sun.

As the time passed, the phone calls home became longer and more frequent as I failed to adjust to my new life. But it was often a really bad phone connection, and the majority of calls were cut short, resulting in even more tears. Most of the calls were reverse charges and this was the beginning of a tradition of particularly expensive phone bills for my parents. Reverse charges back then, a BT chargecard and a satellite phone later. When I read an article in a magazine titled 'Please remember how much I love you when the next phone bill comes through' I couldn't help chuckling to myself as I cut it out to post it to my parents, so that they could read it too.

The democratic elections in South Africa in 1993 were partly linked to the troubles that continued to reign in Lesotho. Daily curfews impacted on us all and prevented us from being outside during the hours of darkness. The noise of the conflict in the distance could be clearly heard in our orphanage. At the same time the Basotho King, Moshoeshoe II. returned to Lesotho after being exiled in the UK. A few days after his return, his daughter, the Princess Constance Christina Maseeiso, died at twenty-five years old. Without really understanding how, I was asked to go to the palace to pay my respects on behalf of Save the Children. This was not an experience I could have ever been prepared for. Two weeks before I left Wales, while I was out celebrating my A level results, one of my close friends was killed in a collision with a lorry. Glesni Wyn Davies – Gles to all of her friends – was seventeen years old with an incredibly bright future ahead of her, and I, like everyone else, failed to understand why one of the most talented, and caring youngsters of our community had been taken away from us so tragically. Whilst sitting in that palace, commiserating with a family that I knew nothing about, I couldn't but fail to realise once again just how precious life is, and how easily it can all be ripped away from us. After Gles's funeral her family gave me a cross made of Welsh gold on a necklace, and to this day I continue to wear it. Just looking at that cross around my neck is the inspiration I need to continue fulfilling each of my dreams while I can.

I met many other volunteers while out in Lesotho, including Geraint Ellis, a family friend of my minister, Mr Ellis. Gwenda, originally from our nearby village Llanuwchllyn, also lived in Johannesburg, which meant I could often visit her for a weekend here and there for a much-needed change of scenery. Another volunteer who became a particularly close friend was Una Finn, an Irish lady who taught in a secondary school there. With close to forty years age difference between us, it was remarkable that we had anything in common, but her youthful spirit and lively personality made her brilliant company, and we shared an amazing holiday travelling through South Africa and Zimbabwe together.

But the *hiraeth* prevailed, and the thought of spending a Christmas away from friends and family was more than I could bear. When I landed back in Manchester airport on Christmas Eve, two months earlier than planned, Mam and Dad were incredibly good in not reminding me of their words of warning before I went. I was too young and too inexperienced to be out there, that was true. But the experience was a significant milestone in my life, and I vowed then that I would never start anything else without committing to completing it, to the end. It made moving to London three months later a much easier hurdle to handle. In line with a lifetime dream, I was about to follow Mam's career – and start my children's nurse training at Great Ormond Street Children's Hospital. My nurse training proved to be the best start that I could have wished for in my adult life, not only for giving me the qualification I needed to pursue a career that I will forever feel passionate about, but also for introducing me to the best group of girls, who became my lifetime friends.

Shortly after my arrival in London I began to play rugby at university and at London Welsh Rugby Club. Although sport had never appeared on the agenda at school I was eager to socialise in an environment that had a Welsh link, and I had always loved watching rugby. At the end of my first season I was selected for the Welsh student squad, and shortly after I was drafted to the Welsh senior squad. To say that I was ecstatic is an understatement, and I was as proud emotionally as I had ever felt when I was given my own red socks and shorts (the only kit provided back then!) before my first game with the A squad. It was overwhelming. It felt like I'd been given the best possible gift in the world.

The years that followed were consumed by everything rugby-related. I moved from London Welsh to London Wasps to join a few of the other Welsh squad players, and to have the opportunity to play at premiership level, which would also help improve the standard of my game.

I precariously balanced my career as a newly-qualified nurse with my rugby ambitions. Simultaneously, I also began to study for a part-time degree in neuroscience, and to plan my wedding to Steve. I'd met Steve soon after arriving in London. He was tall, broad, older, and handsomely dressed in a Royal Navy Petty Officer's uniform! At nineteen I was instantly smitten! Even more so with his willingness to embrace the Welsh culture, support my rugby and to learn the Welsh language – all that was so important to me.

I'd often finish a set of five night shifts on Saturday morning, and skip my break so that I could leave early in order to make it to Cardiff in time for Welsh squad training at 10 am. My essays were written in the car on the way back to London on Saturday night, in time for a club match on Sunday. At the time the set-up and politics in the Welsh

Women's Rugby Union were rather turbulent, and there was a constant turnover of coaching staff and management. Sadly, the coaches who liked my style of play never stayed longer than a season, whereas those who didn't like my style of play stayed for much longer than I would have liked! But under the command of Amanda Bennett in 1999–2000 I was named as the most improved player in the Welsh squad for that season, and was given a weekend treat in Brussels as a reward. In the same season, I was also awarded a financial bursary from Hampshire council (where I lived at the time) to support my travel costs to Cardiff for Welsh squad training. The irony of an English county council supporting me to play rugby for Wales was not lost on me!

I loved my rugby days: the brutality of the physical confrontation in the front row as a prop forward, the discipline required to train when I didn't feel like it, and the importance of a team ethos, not to mention the planning and time-management necessary to make sure I could fit it all in with my other commitments. My nursing experience, and all the usual day-to-day skills nurses use, have also helped me well and truly beyond the hospital walls. My rugby and nursing training certainly helped me in the preparations for the Atlantic. The *London Evening Standard* summed it up well when they ran a full-page spread about me, entitled 'Rugby's Angel shows no mercy – the conversion of children's nurse to leader of the pack'.

Many nurses and rugby players alike live to the ethos of 'work hard, play hard', and I certainly embraced that approach. As it turned out, I only got a 2:2 for my degree, only got A-squad Welsh caps, and ended up being divorced. Many would say that it would have been better if I had focused on doing one thing at a time, and doing it well: I can see that. Maybe I could have a better-class honours in my degree or get selected for a full cap if I had taken that approach. But there's a possibility, of course, that I wouldn't have succeeded any better in either, and then I may never have been able to enjoy and benefit from the other.

Life in London was lively and fun, and my time was spent playing rugby and partying. But amongst all the apparent fun it was particularly difficult to admit, to myself as much as to anyone else, that married life was by now making me desperately unhappy. Issues that seemed unimportant in the naivety of youth became huge burdens, and soon it felt as though I was being suffocated by difficulties and dilemmas I could no longer deal with. In the rural community of Parc, hardly anyone gets divorced, and certainly no one in my family ever had. At times it was impossible to accept my decision to leave Steve, and the guilt would consume me. It took a long time to announce openly that we had separated, and during those incredibly dark and difficult days it was a blessing to be living an invisible and nameless existence in London. A divorce is a sign of failure, after all, and I've never been good at accepting failure – in any aspect of my life.

Given that I was dropped from the Welsh squad and completed my degree at around the same time as my marriage fell apart, it was no surprise that I needed something else to fill my time. Studying for my Masters was an effective therapy, but I still felt a great void. I therefore decided that these changes in my personal situation created the perfect opportunity to re-establish myself, to set myself a new challenge, to do something different – something big ... something *really* big.

I had cycled from Paris to London, which had given me a small taste for adventure. But the prospect of rowing across the Atlantic was on a completely different scale. I couldn't row. I had never been out to sea. But the challenge appealed so much that I could think of nothing else, and the sense of thrill and apprehension filled my heart with more excitement than I had felt in years. It felt as though I was finally being given the ability, once more, to breathe.

3

Race to the start

Things work out best for the people
who make the best out of the way things work out.
Art Linkletter

Shortly after deciding that I wanted to row across the Atlantic I realised that there was a mountain of work ahead of me, just to reach the start line. I had to find a rowing partner that would be willing to join me for the challenge (going it alone would be completely insane, of course); raise £63,000 to fund the trip; learn how to row; buy a suitable boat and equipment; learn the skill of steering and navigating; prepare myself on how to cope with life at sea; and of course fundraise for a charity of my choice.

After leaving Steve, I moved in to live with Herdip Sidhu. Herdip was a senior staff nurse at Great Ormond Street Hospital, and worked on Dickens ward. Dickens ward was also the ward that I would admit the children under my care for their research assessments. Herdip had joined me for the bike ride from Paris to London, and since then we'd got on well, frequently going running and cycling together. She was also single, and without any family responsibility. After very little discussion, she agreed to join me for the voyage.

Very early on the morning of 31 December 2006, with a little less than a year before the start of the race, both of us arrived at Mortlake and Anglia Rowing Club to learn how to row. Ian Roots was a rowing coach there who had family contact with a press worker at the hospital. Crucially, Ian had also rowed across the Atlantic two years previously and was therefore a mine of information, which would help our preparation. After forcing us to row on an *ergo* rowing machine for an hour to get us to row at the same pace he bravely took us out on the Thames for our first outing. Luckily the club had a tub of a boat, named *Hazel*, specifically for the purpose of taking clueless rowers like us out for the first time, and the first outing was a relative success.

After nursing at the hospital for eleven years, I knew for certain that I wanted Great Ormond Street Hospital to be my charity of choice. Herdip felt the same. I had raised funds for the hospital previously, while running a few races like the Great North and Great South Run, and on the cycling trip. But this time, I didn't want the money to go towards the general hospital funds. I had by then specialised as a research nurse, researching the benefits of new emerging drugs, for children suffering from metabolic disorders. Fortunately, the numbers of children that suffer from metabolic diseases known as 'lysosomal storage disorders' are comparatively low, but the rarity of the disease makes raising awareness of the disorders, and funds for research to find a cure, practically impossible. I therefore felt passionately that a challenge of this kind was appropriate, not only to raise money but also to raise awareness of what these children endure on a day-to-day basis.

Persuading the 'powers that be' in the charity that the money should be ring-fenced for metabolic research was much harder than I had imagined. Indeed, even persuading the charity that the challenge wasn't beyond their scope was very difficult; they were reluctant, to say the least. In a bid to gain support, Herdip and I arranged a meeting with Dr Jane

Collins, the Chief Executive of the hospital, to try to get her to back us. I wore my reading glasses for the meeting in the hope that it helped make me seem sensible and wise! I needn't have worried: 'Will you be doing it naked?' was her first question! She was clearly well-informed about one of the most crucial aspects of our challenge ahead! Getting her support was crucial to our campaign, and soon afterwards some of the key pieces began to come together, suggesting at last that we could really start planning for the challenge ahead.

Despite the obvious concerns of investing in such an ambitious high-risk challenge, the charity agreed to pay for the boat in the short term to give us more time to find a sponsor. This made the campaign open to heavy criticism if it all went wrong and placed even more pressure on us to ensure that we would succeed and make the investment worthwhile. But this was a risk we had to accept if we had any chance of being ready in time for the beginning of the race.

The campaign by now seemed to me like a snowball. Pretty soon after sharing our dream, announcing it publicly and starting the preparation, the snowball started to roll, and was growing at a pace that I could never have imagined. Even on those uncertain moments, when doubts about the challenge ahead raised their head, and my desire to continue on the quest to fulfil my dream was a little shaken, the snowball grew and ran at such a pace that even if I had really wanted to change my mind and not go, I don't think I would have been able to.

When people heard about my planned adventure the majority couldn't possibly comprehend why anyone would choose to do it, and I received many negative comments. 'Crazy', 'stupid' and 'idiotic' were some of the friendliest comments, and early on the negative responses and the attempts to ridicule or belittle our efforts began to irritate me. It seemed that some people just couldn't be happy, or even accept seeing others trying to live their dreams. But on reflection, all those negative and sometimes insulting comments were like money in the bank, an investment for the difficult times that I could later rely on to give me strength and determination to press on and persevere.

Understandably, I guess, most people didn't think that we had a chance in hell! We were completely inexperienced, and that was clearly evident in our preparation. But one can never underestimate the power of determination. And aside from the majority, there did appear a handful of angels that went out of their way to help us in our campaign. The two angels that shone the brightest were Lucy Jameson and Jo Bardoe. Both Lucy and Jo have children who suffer from a metabolic disorder, but in the midst of their worries and woes both decided to help support us. The campaign was very close to their hearts, obviously, which I hope gave them the strength to help us endlessly in the middle of their busy day-to-day lives. Mia, Jo's daughter, was one of the children under my care who had consented to test a new medication being developed to stop, or at least slow, the rate of disease progression. But after three years of trying, and endless assessments, we had to accept the fact that the drug was worthless. The disappointment was enormous for everyone involved, and the future looked very uncertain once again. By sharing these daily experiences with them I had become close to them as a family.

We were venturing across the Atlantic Ocean as competitors in the Woodvale Challenge, a race the organisers had christened 'The World's Toughest Rowing Race'. The first race had been held in 1997, and before then less than ten people had rowed across the Atlantic Ocean. Since 1997 the race had become a bi-annual event, and created much public interest when Olympic gold-medal rower James Cracknell and TV presenter Ben Fogle completed the race in 49 days, 19 hours and 8 minutes. That race was also well-known because six of the twenty boats competing had to be rescued after capsizing in heavy weather. It wasn't difficult to understand why more people had climbed to the heights of Everest, and been out to space, than had rowed across the Atlantic.

Woodvale also designed and constructed the boats for the crossing. But when I ordered ours, I still felt a tiny bit apprehensive, knowing that there would only be 8 millimetres of marine plywood between me and the depths of the big blue sea! Soon after we paid Woodvale Events for the boat they went into administration, increasing the pressure upon us in our battle with all the doubting Thomases. Although Simon Chalk, the company director reassured us that the race would go ahead, and that the company would be re-established as Woodvale Challenge, we were still worried that we'd lose our boat – even though it was still merely an empty shell. Given the pressure, I took the decision that it was best to take the boat in its unfinished state and pay another boat-builder to complete the work. However, the number of boat-builders that specialise in ocean-rowing boats is much lower than the number of people that choose to row an ocean!

Luckily, Lucy had arranged for us to be able to use the facilities of the Hayling Island Sailing Club, on the Solent in Hampshire. It's a thriving club with amazing facilities, and through Lucy's persuasive skills and the club's generosity it was agreed that we could keep the boat there for free to practice on the Solent – as soon as the boat was ready! Like an answer to our prayers, there was a small company by the name of Dolphin Quays, based in nearby Emsworth, who had already worked on two other similar ocean-rowing boats. Considering their location they were the perfect choice to complete the work on our boat.

Herdip, who is a Sikh, was in India being blessed at the Golden Temple when Simon Chalk drove our boat up to Hayling Island. It was an empty, grey shell, and according to Lucy, who was there with me to greet him, I was a whiter shade of grey myself when I saw how small it actually was. Tim from Dolphin Quays joined us for the arrival to assess how much work was left to be done – and to confirm that it could all be done in the precious time that we now had left before the race.

While Tim and his colleague Richard started on the work of preparing the boat, Herdip and I were still facing the insurmountable problem of lack of money. Many had warned us that funding the campaign would be as challenging as the row itself, and we were slowly realising how true that was. Building and equipping the boat alone would now cost around £25,000–30,000, not to mention other additional costs such as shipping, insurance and the freeze-dried food. With less than a year to go, we weren't even a step closer to finding a sponsor.

A designer from the charity office in the hospital had named our campaign 'Nautical Nurses', and we were very pleased with the message it conveyed and the logo that was designed to go with it. But despite the catchy name and the worthy cause, the challenge was far too expensive and far too ambitious to persuade any company to invest in us at the necessary level. The only promising contact we had was Ollie, a friend of Charles Denton, the Chief Executive of the charity. Ollie was a businessman who had competed in the

ARC sailing race across the Atlantic, and seemed to be a promising potential sponsor for us. After an initial meeting, Ollie decided that he would take us out on a sailing trip across the Channel. In May, therefore, seven months before the start of the race, Herdip and I drove down to Southampton to experience our first ever outing to sea!

Within hours of being at sea, the wind and waves increased and most of the crew became seasick. Luckily, I didn't suffer – I must have a stomach like one of Dad's cows! I had a brilliant opportunity, therefore, to find my 'sea legs' and to have a go at helming the boat while using the compass and GPS to direct the way. We also worked in two-hour shifts, which gave us a chance to experience the routine that would face us on the Atlantic. But Ollie's yacht was pure luxury compared to our boat, and within 24 hours we'd moored in Sandbanks and were enjoying a hot shower and a lovely home-cooked meal. Unfortunately, Herdip suffered really badly with seasickness throughout. She felt so bad that she couldn't take part in many of the activities.

Two days after the sailing trip I spoke to Ollie on the phone. He said he wouldn't be investing in our campaign. If I changed rowing partners, and found somebody else other than Herdip, he may reconsider, but as it stood he didn't foresee that we had any chance of success. With less than seven months to go until the start of the race, and two weeks until our launch party things were looking very glum. But I couldn't consider Ollie's conditions. Herdip was a friend, as much a part of this campaign as I was by then, and to be honest I knew that I would struggle to find a suitable partner to join me in time for the start anyway. Understandably Ollie's opinion broke Herdip's heart; it was a devastating blow to her self-confidence, and one that probably had far-reaching consequences. But even though I tried my best to reassure her that I had full confidence in her ability, quietly a stream of doubts began to emerge in my mind too. However, with the launch party quickly approaching there was no option but to battle on with a brave face, and ignore the niggling concerns. It was one thing for others to doubt our strengths and chances of success, but we had to be completely confident in our own ability.

Hayling Island Sailing Club was once again extremely supportive of our campaign, and with Lucy's help had arranged a launch party to coincide with a sailing race at the club, so despite the recent blow we had to enjoy the day.

The bank holiday arrived with its usual weather of wind and rain. I travelled to Hayling Island the night before with my closest friend Karen and her husband Duncan. Mam and Dad also drove all the way down from north Wales to support the event. I had told my parents about my ambition to row across the Atlantic back in December. It had been an incredibly difficult experience to try and explain to them, and to justify why I wanted to do it, particularly knowing how much they would worry for me. Even though they didn't understand, and weren't particularly happy about it, they were always completely supportive.

The Chaplain from the hospital and the Sikh leader had also travelled all the way down to bless the boat and to wish us well on our voyage. Through a competition for the children in the hospital we had chosen a name for the boat, and there, during the service, with champagne and sacred water from the Golden Temple, the boat was christened *Dream Maker*. This was the boat that would make the dream of rowing the Atlantic come true for Herdip and me – but more importantly, it would hopefully lead towards fulfilling the dream of the children that suffered from metabolic disorder by advancing the knowledge through research that would be funded by our efforts, knowledge that ultimately, we hoped, would go towards identifying a cure for their suffering.

Personally I was delighted with the name *Dream Maker*. The initials D.M were the same as Taid, my Dad's Dad, David Morris. Most people referred to Taid as D.M, and even though he had passed away a few years previously it was particularly reassuring for me to know that he would be travelling with me in name, as well as in spirit.

Two days after the launch party Jo Bardoe called me. Her family friend, a Chief Executive for a large company in the city, was going to sponsor us! Jamie Hopkins, from Mapeley Ltd, was just like Prince Charming galloping on a white horse to save us, and within days we had a cheque of £63,000 to pay the costs! The boat's name was already leading the way.

The following weeks and months sped past at pace that I couldn't keep up with. Completion of the boat was running desperately behind schedule, and every day was a battle. It required numerous phone calls and hundreds of emails to chase things up. It was a full-time job to keep track of all the arrangements, which of course wasn't possible given that both Herdip and I worked full-time as it was. Sometimes I'd look in on my life from the outside, and see it race past at a hundred and ten miles per hour, without any pit stops! The stress of keeping all the arrangements ticking over caused a lot of tension – with the workers at Dolphin Quays, with the workers at the charity office who were in charge of ordering the equipment, and sometimes with Herdip. I sensed that both Dolphin Quays and the staff at the charity were avoiding my calls – knowing that I wouldn't stop with the nagging until I knew that all the work were being completed. I was worse than a dog with a bone!

With so much work left to be done on the boat before it would be ready and with no hope of going out practicing on the Solent for a while longer, both of us were left to train on ergo rowing machines at the gym and the occasional morning rowing on the Thames. By then I'd also made contact with Poplar rowing club in east London through Rowan Watson, one of the members. Rowan had close contacts with Parc, and was incredibly supportive.

Most people, when asking about our planning, would consider only the physical training aspect of our preparation. The physical training was of course crucially important, and required a lot of time and commitment to ensure that we would be fit enough to row for twelve hours a day and strong enough to pull the para-anchor in from the water. Herdip was brilliant at spending hours on end on the *ergo*, but I'd get easily bored of looking at myself in the mirror rowing away hour after hour – especially when there was so much work left to be done. I couldn't ignore the fact that being fit and strong would be pointless if we didn't have a boat and equipment to row in!

To ensure that there was variety in our training programme, and to avoid the boredom of the *ergo*, we mixed the rowing with running and weight-lifting. I enjoyed them so much more than the rowing alone. Herdip and I ran a few 10 km races and half-marathons in the year up to the race, before entering for the Snowdon marathon. On a beautiful autumn day, the Welsh landscape shone through, and despite the steep climbs and difficult terrain I enjoyed every minute. Being able to run most of it pretty much on my own, rather than cramped with hundreds of other runners, made it even more special. The contrast with the London marathon five months later couldn't have been greater. I hated every step of that one – despite having raised lots of money for the Gaucher Association.

The compulsory courses that were part of the race rules – the RYA Ocean Yachtmaster, VHF radio licence, and sea survival – were another crucial aspect of the training. And even though both of us were nurses, a 'first aid at sea' course was also compulsory. The RYA Ocean Yachtmaster theory course was difficult as I found the mathematical equations particularly challenging. Luckily *Pura Vida*, another crew who were competing in the same race, were also taking the course at the same time as us. Tom, John, Carl and Robbie, along with Scott and Neil from *Ocean Summit*, who we met on the other courses, became good friends who supported us not only on the courses, but while preparing in La Gomera, while rowing the ocean, and much later while adjusting to life back on land.

Finally *Dream Maker* was ready for a trial run out on the Solent – and not a second too soon. Even though conditions on the Solent were nothing like those that awaited us on the Atlantic, it was the best thing that we could have arranged for training and much more than we could cope with at that time! Our lack of knowledge in reading the charts, and our lack of power behind the oars, meant that the tide frequently pushed us into trouble. We were useless, and there was no denying it. We were completely reliant on Frank from the sailing club and his rescue boat. Even after numerous rescues, however, Frank never once said a cross or negative word – just a gentle word of advice on how to avoid similar troubles again. He was unbelievably supportive, and without him and Mike Baker, one of the club's trustees, we would never even have managed to leave the banks of Hayling Island. Mike spent numerous hours driving *Dream Maker* backwards and forwards from the sailing club to Dolphin Quays, getting his feet wet on more than one occasion while putting the boat in the water. Time after time, I couldn't believe how Mike and Frank, who were complete strangers to us previously, would volunteer their time and energy to endlessly support us. In this busy world that we live in, it was a miracle that we were receiving such support, and it was their commitment, along with that of a few others, that became the foundation to our successful crossing.

After much waiting, and yet far too soon, it was October and time to pack *Dream Maker* and all the equipment ready to be sent out to La Gomera. The hero of the hour was Dad – who drove all the way from Parc to Hayling Island before risking driving *Dream Maker* through the streets of London. Pulling an 8-metre trailer with such a precious cargo through the streets of London is quite a feat! But it was all worth it so that our co-workers and the children in the hospital could have the opportunity to see the boat for the last time before we headed off. In the relief of finding a volunteer (without too much persuasion, even) I hadn't considered the responsibility that was on poor Dad's shoulders! I wonder now whether he ever considered taking one of the corners too quickly in the hope that *Dream Maker* would take a tumble – putting an end to this latest whim of mine!

Around seventy people gathered to see *Dream Maker* in the square outside the hospital, and with an announcement by Dr Jane Collins, our campaign was live on London news. There was no turning back now! Very early the next morning Dad, Mam, Herdip and I started on the trip to Newark in central England to pack *Dream Maker* safely in a container ship, ready to be transported to the start line. Finally, all the efforts and planning had come together.

*Only those who risk going too far
can possibly find out how far one can go.*
T. S. Eliot

Amongst all the hours of planning, it was surprising that my career existed, let alone progressed. While studying for my Masters I had developed a new format for assessing children with Neuronopathic Gaucher disease – a metabolic disease that slowly causes damage to the brain, and a disease that many of the children under my care suffered from. My work won a prize in an international conference, was later published, and led to interest by two different pharmaceutical companies that were developing new drugs in the field. Unbelievably, I signed a contract with both companies to do further research into the value of the assessment tool, and other potential outcome measures of the disease. Most importantly, the contract would enable me to register for a part-time PhD. Dr Ashok Vellodi and Professor Robert Surtees, two doctors I had known for years, and whom I respected greatly, agreed to be my supervisors. A PhD would be a commitment for over three years, but I felt it was a worthwhile investment for my future career, and a commitment that would give me something to focus on when I returned from the row. I always think it's important to have a long-term plan. There is always a bit of a downer after completing a challenge, a kind of mourning where one thinks, 'What on earth do I do now?' It's better to try to circumvent the void by having another project in mind, and for me, my PhD would be my next project.

While attending another international conference, I listened to a presentation by Dr Agnés Saint Raymond, head of sector at the European Medicine Agency. Agnés was a key member in the development of a new regulation in Europe that would force pharmaceutical companies to assess the safety and efficacy of all drugs in children from now on, a profile which can be very different to that seen in adults. Following my clinical and research experience I knew that the regulation would lead to much-needed changes in the provision of child health, and improvements that were very much overdue.

A week after the conference I emailed a copy of my CV to Agnés, expressing my interest in working in the field in the future, if an opportunity ever presented itself. I never dreamt that I actually had a chance of securing work there, but I felt that I had nothing to lose by expressing an interest. It was a complete shock when I was later invited for an interview and an even greater surprise when I was offered a position within the newly established paediatric team in the European Medicine Agency. I could hardly speak a word of French, and even though English was my second language, my mother-tongue being Welsh, two official European languages are required to work there (frustratingly, Welsh has not yet been given official language status in Europe). I needed a day a week off work to continue with my PhD studies, and there was, of course, the minor detail that I was soon to disappear off to sea for a few months! I was over the moon to be given such an amazing opportunity in my career, and could hardly contain myself. In the middle of August therefore, less than four months before I was due to head off across the waves, I left Great Ormond Street Hospital after twelve years of service to embark on a new career.

I genuinely just couldn't believe it all. I had found a sponsor for our rowing campaign, secured support to study for a PhD, and had been offered a position in a key organisation that would influence the health of children in

Europe. I was flying on a high of success, while simultaneously sinking in fear of the disappointment that was sure to follow! Such an unbelievable amount of luck in a period of three months was not possible! I was certain that a big disappointment, or a crashing fall, was sure to happen, and the worry weighed like a heavy rock in the pit of my stomach. Maybe it's a side-effect of being a Welsh rugby supporter living in London in the mid nineties ... the first half of every match would look promising, and Neil Jenkins would often kick us into the lead. Hopes for a win would be high, but then the last quarter would always turn into a disaster, and the opposition (most often England) would trample over us. I prayed every minute of every day that such a defeat or a disastrous loss would not come my way – not while out at sea, at least!

The last few days in the UK were one mad rush. There just seemed to be so much to do. I had a friend living in my flat while out at sea, so I didn't have to worry about my home, at least. But the last-minute list of things to pack and things to do seemed endless.

Apart from an early Christmas lunch with my family, around two weeks before I flew out to La Gomera, we hadn't organised a leaving party. Neither Herdip nor I were keen to have one. I had cried more than enough while saying my goodbyes to Karen and Duncan as it was. And saying our goodbyes to Jamie Hopkins had also been harder than I had anticipated. Since signing the massive cheque Jamie had gone out of his way to support us. He'd even arranged for Chris Moon, a motivational speaker who had lost an arm and a leg in a landmine explosion, to help us prepare psychologically for the challenge ahead. But while saying goodbye to Jamie in a private club in London, while Vivienne Westwood and her friends partied next to us, I felt like the weight of the world was pressing on my shoulders. This was no longer a personal (ad)venture. So many people had invested their time and money to support us that I knew that to fail would result in so much more than just a personal disappointment to us. Numerous other people would also be disappointed. Jamie gave us both a parting gift, a Links-of-London bracelet with the words 'Always believe in yourself, Jamie' engraved on them. The bracelet was a perfect gift, and a symbol of the support of everybody who would be travelling with us across every mile of the way.

They always say that time changes things,
But you actually have to change them yourself.
Andy Warhol

Arriving in La Gomera was a huge relief, an escape from the daily obligation of life in London, and finally an opportunity to concentrate completely on the journey ahead – without any distraction from work, studying or any of my other commitments.

La Gomera is one of the smallest islands in the Canaries. It's around the same size as the Isle of Man, and formed of volcanic rocks that rise steeply from the clear blue Atlantic. The normally quiet harbour of San Sebastián and its usual tranquillity was transformed with the arrival of all the competitors arriving to prepare for the race start. It was from the isle of La Gomera that Christopher Columbus departed for his voyage in 1492 – without knowing what awaited him over the horizon. In San Sebastián there is a small chapel where, according to the tales, Columbus said a final prayer before leaving. Naturally, I had to be sure to maintain the tradition.

The atmosphere in San Sebastián was magical and electrifying. The last few days of preparation were fun-filled, and action-packed, with excitement, tears, hard work and fear all rolled into one. We were surrounded by others who had the exact same aspirations as us, shared our dream and our desire to cross successfully. I got a real buzz from being out there, but just like everyone else I was completely on edge waiting for the adventure ahead.

Everyone worked long hours to make sure that everything was done, checked, and checked again in order to be ready. The race rules were clear on the type of equipment that had to be on board, and the amount of food that had to be packed. Every boat was carefully scrutineered by the race organisers to make sure that every one of the crews complied.

Compared to some of the other crews, we were actually reasonably well-organised, thankfully, but even so we had enough to do. Packing 6,000 calories each a day for ninety days was a challenge in itself. But crucially our life raft was missing a Solas B pack, which is necessary for ocean crossings as it contains additional survival equipment necessary for off-shore survival. With San Sebastián being so small it was impossible to access such technical equipment out there, so we had to rely heavily on the staff in the charity office to source them back in the UK before finding a way of transporting them out there to us. Slowly, one by one, things were getting sorted as our imminent departure date got closer and closer.

On 30 November, three days before the race start date Mam, Dad and Gles arrived to wave us off. Despite being very grateful that they were there to support me, amongst all the preparation and the race meetings with Woodvale I just couldn't relax and enjoy time in their company.

On the eve of the race, while Mam, Dad and Gles stood around waiting for the 'last supper', Herdip and I were in a state of complete panic! While trying to set the first few way-points on our Global Positioning System (GPS) I'd inadvertently managed to wipe all the basic settings. With the help of Chris Martin, who'd rowed across the Atlantic solo and was planning a world first row across the Pacific Ocean, we set about reading every single page in the manual to re-set it all. Without a GPS we wouldn't be going anywhere! I certainly didn't fancy my chances going with a sextant.

Finally, the four of us sat down to enjoy a tasty pizza, while Herdip spent the time with her brother and sister. Shortly after I fell asleep, much easier than I had expected – in a warm, dry, still bed for the last time for a considerable number of weeks.

Time stood still on the race morning. After I had packed everything, and given my parents an enormous bag of my belongings to take back to Wales, the four of us sat in the square in San Sebastián to eat a late breakfast. My mouth was bone dry and my mind preoccupied as I tried to force myself to swallow a cheese and ham sandwich and to enjoy some fresh food for the last time.

Everyone sensed the tension as they watched the clock tick down towards midday. Dad and I went to sit on *Dream Maker* to rearrange a thing or two. We were joined by Pete van Kets, one of the South African contestants rowing in *Gquma Challenger* for one more goodbye. Even though I'd only known Pete and his rowing partner Bill Godfrey barely two weeks, both had been incredibly friendly and supportive in helping us plan our route across, and prepare for the weather we'd face in the first few days. Pete took Dad by the hand and said 'You've got a very brave daughter'. My heart skipped a beat. At that moment, the last thing I felt was brave.

Hugs, best wishes, good-byes, words of advice and encouragement, photo after photo, all in one never-ending circle until I just had to escape the marina and everyone else to hide on Dream Maker. While pushing the boat out away from the harbour wall for the last time it was much easier to hide all emotions behind sun glasses.

If you are going through hell, keep going.
Winston Churchill

At twelve o'clock on 2 December a fog horn marked the beginning of the race. Twenty-two rowing boats embarking on a challenge of a lifetime, and a harbour that was buzzing with anticipation. But within three hours, with the waves increasing in size, we couldn't see any of the other boats. Pretty soon Herdip was seasick. Thankfully, she felt better when rowing rather than resting, which meant that we could continue to alternate with the rowing, changing over every two hours, as planned.

The first night was like a wet, cold, extremely dark nightmare. This was by far the most unbearable night of my life, and coming out to row the following morning wasn't much better. Both of us were now starting to feel the physical impact of rowing for nearly twenty-four hours without eating. Although I wasn't seasick, I had no appetite whatsoever.

One of the main side effects of the seasickness patches that we were using is an extremely dry mouth. As a result it was pretty impossible to chew on anything. Sleep deprivation by now was also playing a part in making me feel nauseous. Thankfully we'd packed a couple of tins of pineapple and peaches in juice, and this was the only thing I could manage to swallow on that first day.

Early morning on the second day, news came through that *Titanic Challenge,* one of the other boats, was out of the race already. One of the crew had fallen overboard and had been in the water for forty-five minutes waiting to be rescued. Luckily, he was unharmed, but was left too frightened to continue with the race. It was a stark reminder of how quickly it could all be over – in more ways than one.

As we sat there feeling pretty depressed, Herdip nearly jumped off her seat as she spotted a pod of around twenty dolphins swimming within fifteen metres of our boat. It seemed like the dolphins had sensed our low spirits and swam by to give us some moral support. It was an unbelievable boost – momentarily. But out there on the ocean, emotions change within matters of seconds, and often with no apparent reason. While watching those dolphins showcasing their jumps we were on top of the world, ecstatic with the uniqueness of our situation. But seconds later, as the dolphins disappeared to the depths below our spirits sank with them.

Thirty-six hours into the race Herdip continued to be seasick, but I couldn't have foreseen the effect the sickness would have on her. She decided that if she didn't feel better soon that she wouldn't be able to continue. Even though I had thought of nothing much else since leaving the harbour walls, to hear it said out loud was completely different. Once a declaration of that magnitude has been made it's impossible to avoid the issue. It lingers in the air, suffocating any other small-talk. Sadly, the wind hadn't snatched the sentence away, and I could concentrate on nothing else. Later, following intense discussions I managed to persuade her to stay on the boat for one full week. One full week should be long enough for the seasickness to subside, and if we had to give up at that point, a week would also be a little bit more respectable, to show people at home that we'd given it our best shot, at least.

The following nights were equally as miserable, and adjusting to rowing in pitch darkness was getting no easier. Without being able to see which direction the waves travelled from we couldn't prepare for them, so wave after wave washed over us. With sleep deprivation now a crippling curse we struggled to stay awake during our rowing shift, and found it impossible to stay warm. The temperature dropped considerably after sunset, so we shivered continuously as a result of being consistently wet. Because of our lack of confidence in the dark we decided to concentrate on steering the boat only, leaving the prevailing currents to carry us rather than row. Although this made us feel safer in terms of safety, sitting there for two hours, not generating any body heat through rowing made us suffer even more from the cold. To help, we decided to wear our survival suits. Even today, I just can't imagine how anyone could get into one of those quickly in an emergency. It was a challenge and a half to get into it, made even harder when we were rolling around in the confines of the small cabin. There was no point in bothering to try to get out of it during breaktimes, because there would be no time left to sleep before having to start on the process of getting it back on. But for those two hours, while sitting out on deck, my head down to avoid the constant flow of salty water crashing over me, it was the survival suits that kept me going. It was some kind of bonus at that time that we couldn't eat or drink much, and therefore were too dehydrated to need the toilet very often.

Sleep deprivation proved itself to be an unbearable curse. It was near impossible to stay awake while rowing at night, but watching the red compass light haunt us as it

The day of my christening, summer 1976, with Mam and Dad, and (left to right) Meilir, Glesni and Dylan, who looks particularly happy to welcome his new little sister!

A promising farmer's daughter in my early days!

The start of my interest in sports – a new bike from Father Christmas

Me in July 2011, the new Dr Elin Haf Davies!
(Photo: Keith Mills)

All my nieces and nephews in their Ocean Angels T-shirts

Support from Non, Heledd and Sara at the start of the Bala triathlon

The start of the second day of the desert race – one of three Welsh competitors

Proud of wearing the national red rugby shirt of Wales with Sian Williams, Wales A centre (Photo: Kevin Mills)

Blackheath, London, in July 2006, after biking from Paris in three and a half days – the first adventure I had with Herdip

The finish of the desert race, near the pyramids

The start of the Nautical Nurses campaign

My farewell supper (and early Christmas dinner!) with my family and Rhun, my godson, before the Atlantic trip

Gwion, Dafydd and Catrin, my brother Dylan's children, with Dream Maker.

Rowing under a rainbow! Very happily rowing Dream Maker
across the Atlantic Ocean

Celebrating Christmas Day in Dream Maker, *on the Atlantic Ocean, with a visit by
the boat* Kilkullen

Dad, Gles and Mam welcoming me with the Welsh flag at Nelson Dock, Antigua, 17 February 2008

An emotional reunion for all in Antigua

A grin of relief having landed in Antigua, after seventy-seven days rowing the Atlantic Ocean

Herdip and me hugging after landing in Antigua

Waving the Welsh flag in Antigua, seconds before standing on dry land for the first time

Big smile! Seeing Nain for the first time after finishing the journey across the Atlantic

With Dad, my sister Gles, and Ilan Aled, her son, on the top of Snowdon – a family day to celebrate my return from crossing the Atlantic.

Jo Bardoe, Jamie Hopkins, Mia Bardoe, Lucy Jameson and Henry Jameson at Gatwick airport, welcoming me home from the Atlantic crossing – five people who were essential to the campaign

At the start line of the Indian Ocean race, 19 April 2009, with two of the nine other competitors.

The 'Angels' taking a break

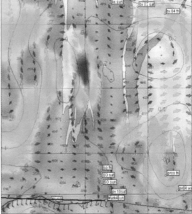

Three 'Angels' enjoying the Indian Ocean

The weather forecast and our position, the end of April 2009, on the Indian Ocean. Green indicates fair weather, and the red colour denotes an area to avoid

Jumping into the Indian Ocean to relax in the hot weather!

Rowing on the quiet sea

Enjoying the Indian Ocean

The changeable skies of the Indian Ocean, with an array of beautiful colours

Enjoying a chance to sunbathe in the luxury of Pura Vida

A squall approaching

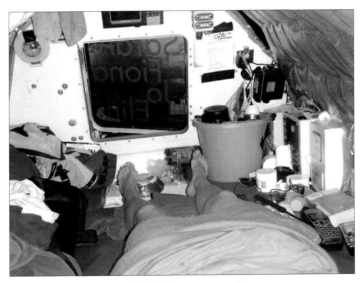

Pura Vida's *luxurious stern cabin*

Swimming in the Indian Ocean,
hundreds of miles from land!

The stern cabin hatch of Pura Vida, with loads of pictures of our families and
friends that provided us with many hours of amusement

Pura Vida without her crew on the Indian Ocean

A huge ship on the near horizon – the cause of a few nightmares and great fear!

Having a rest from rowing on Pura Vida

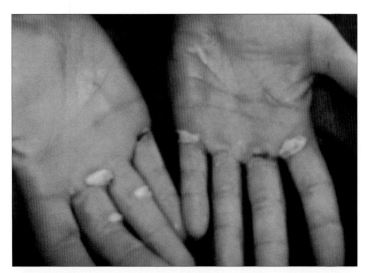

Painfully blistered hands in the early days because of all the rowing

The sun rises, giving us a huge boost after the long dark nights

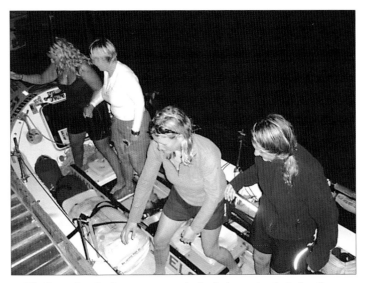

The Ocean Angels *about to step onto dry land after rowing the Indian Ocean for over seventy-eight days*

With Sara Fflur, Ilan Aled and Sarah after landing in Mauritius, and enjoying fresh fruit for the first time in eleven weeks

The Ocean Angels *on the beach in Mauritius,*
celebrating after setting two world records

September 2009: receiving an award for services to Wales, from the then First
Minister, Rhodri Morgan, after returning from the Indian Ocean crossing

formed various shapes in front of our tired eyes was equally traumatic. But when breaktime came, I couldn't completely relax enough to sleep then either. The waves crashed against the cabin with such force that the noise sounded like an express train crashing into us. And even if I could have slept through the noise, being thrown across the cabin was sure to wake me!

In those early days Herdip would often call on me during my break to help her if a flying fish had landed on the deck, or if she was unsure about the bearing we were taking. And at that time, she also asked me to sleep with the hatch a little bit ajar as she understandably felt a bit apprehensive alone on deck, at night. Even when asleep, therefore, I think that I was always trying to be 'on watch'. My dreams were so vivid that I would often imagine that I had heard Herdip call that it was time to swap over. Frequently I'd roll out of the sleeping bag and into my wet clothes ready to take the oars only to discover that I'd only been asleep fifteen minutes. The sleep deprivation was so extreme, and debilitating that even after staring at my watch for several minutes I would still have no comprehension of how much time I had left on my break.

By the third day Herdip was still retching, and hadn't eaten anything worthwhile since we'd left land. The heat of the mid-day sun was also unbearable, so both of us were now starting to worry about her physical well-being, and wanted to do something to prevent her from deteriorating further. To take advantage of the fact that we were both nurses we had packed an extra supply of medical kit, containing needles, stronger medication and fluids for intravenous use. Both of us felt that it would be sensible therefore to give Herdip some intravenous fluids to stop her from getting dehydrated any further. My nurse training hadn't prepared me to find a vein while rocking back and forth on a rowing boat in the middle of the Atlantic! But with some luck I managed to find one, and inject a stronger anti-emetic and some fluids containing sugar and salts into Herdip's vein. It was a huge relief, and soon enough she did seem to be feeling a bit better. Unfortunately, however, one of the side-effect of the stronger drug that I'd given her is hallucinations, and she gave us both a fright that night when she insisted that she could see a soldier sitting on the oar!

With Herdip's condition as it was, I was forcing myself to eat and drink regularly to be sure that one of us at least had the strength and well being to push on. Chocolate had never been so important in my life before, and I came to appreciate the concept of eating to live, rather than living to eat. No mean feat for someone like me, who had previously attached so much importance to eating generally!

On that third night, while we were slowly getting accustomed to the extreme darkness, a cruise ship appeared on the horizon. Within minutes the ship appeared to be literally beside us, and for a while we were convinced that it was aiming straight for us. One of the biggest fears for any ocean rower is having a collision with one of those big cruise or cargo ships. Even though the odds must be pretty small out there in the expanse of the ocean, it has happened, and everyone knows that such a collision would be catastrophic, and not just to the chances of continuing with the crossing.

One of the most important pieces of kit that we had on board was a 'Sea-Me'. The Sea-Me identifies a radar signal from any nearby ships, before amplifying it and transmitting it back to inform them that we are there – implying that we are somewhat bigger than we actually are. Since we are so small, and low on the water line, it's not feasible to expect anyone to see us. Frequently, we'd be much lower and smaller than the waves around us. The Sea-Me would therefore warn us with an alarm, which would ring louder and more frequently the closer each ship would be to us.

On average, most cargo ships travel at around eighteen to twenty knots, and therefore from seeing a ship on the horizon, around three miles away, there are only about nine minutes until the time of possible collision. We rowed at an average of two knots an hour; nowhere near fast enough to be able to row out of anyone's way. The best option, therefore, was to avoid getting too close to them at all, and if you feared that they *were* too close, taking into account the risk of the after-wash as well, the best thing was to try to contact the ship with the VHF radio and ask the captain to change course slightly. But that night, as we looked at the cruise ship getting closer we couldn't make any contact with the ship. Fear started to set in, made worse from knowing that these ships can potentially be unmanned and cruising on auto-pilot. Our next option was to set off a white flare into the night sky in a bid to warn them that we were there. If we'd been remotely experienced, and hadn't let the panic set in, we would by that point have realised that the ship would be passing us with plenty of distance to spare, saving us much time and much emotion as we frantically searched our deck for the right flare.

During those first days we relied heavily on our para-anchor. In hindsight it was probably because of our lack of confidence to really push on. The para-anchor is like a large parachute, attached to a rope and a trip-line with a buoy on it. Once out in the water the parachute would fill up with water, a couple of waves away from the boat, and the weight of that water trapped in the parachute would work like an anchor, stopping us from being pushed backwards by the wind. Unfortunately it didn't work so effectively for us all the time, especially if we were caught in an area where the currents were strong in the direction we didn't want to travel. It was often a bit of a guessing game, and a lot of pot luck as to whether we deployed it in the right conditions. Our lack of experience once again meant that we were spending hours deploying it and then pulling it back in, time after time. Even with the help of the trip-line it still required brute force to be able to pull it back in, especially in rough weather where we were being thrown around on the deck. To make matters even worse, now and again a big wave would pull it away from us, ripping the rope through our already sore hands – and adding to the number of sores and bleeding blisters on them.

With so much rope and a long trip-line attached, it was easy to get completely confused as to which part went where, and losing sight of each end. It was a skill in itself to know how to throw it overboard upwind, and guessing how far away from the boat to allow it to drag. If the wind changed direction quickly, and that seemed to happen pretty much all the time, it would all blow back towards you, making everything into one knotted mess.

That was what happened one day in the first week. Within minutes of deploying it we noticed that it had somehow managed to tangle itself around the rudder. With the force of the wind blowing us against the weight of the para-anchor I was worried that the rudder would be ripped off. That, of course, would have been a pretty big disaster in terms of our ability to steer without one! We tried each way we could to untangle it from the rudder, but to no avail. Cutting through the rope with one of the knives on deck was starting to appear as the only choice, but that would mean continuing without a para-anchor, and we didn't really want that either. At that time, I felt that our only choice was to jump into the water and to work under the boat to release the rope from the rudder. Herdip didn't like the idea: the sea was rough, and going for a swim at that time was far from being a sensible option. But I just couldn't see any other way of stopping either the rudder or the para-anchor ending up at the bottom of the sea bed.

Therefore I jumped into the sea, and felt the coldness of the water permeate my bones. Whoever said that fast-moving water is warm hadn't been in the mid-Atlantic during a storm, I thought! I held on tightly to the rope that was tied to the side of the boat. With wave after wave throwing us in every direction I could feel the complete weight of the boat pulling heavily through my elbows. I worked my way to the stern to reach the rudder, before holding my breath and diving underneath *Dream Maker*. With my diving goggles on I could see everything, and I started on the task of untangling the rope, while holding on tightly to it at the same time. The leash that was attached to my ankle to stop me from being dragged away from the boat was too short to allow me to reach, so I undid it, relying completely on my grip on the boat to stop me from being engulfed by the large waves.

Finally, I managed to release the para-anchor from the rudder. I was breathless and completely exhausted, and struggled to climb back on to the safety of the deck, thankfully with both rudder and para-anchor still intact and on board.

You are never given a wish
without also being given the power to make it true.
You may have to work for it, however.
Richard Bach

Although things hadn't been as bad as the first night, things weren't improving massively either. To make things worse, some of our equipment was already faulty, or had stopped working altogether. The light on the compass had stopped working within three days, and I had forgotten to pack spare batteries for us. I cursed our stupidity for not choosing a compass that was powered by our solar panels. After nine days our light igniters for the gas stove stopped working too – because of the dampness in the cabin, all our electrical equipment was being temperamental. Obviously food was one of the most important commodities out there, and without boiling water to prepare our freeze-dried rations it didn't look too promising for us for the rest of the journey.

Like every other boat crew we had to be completely self-sufficient for the duration of the crossing to be ranked within the race rules. Asking for supplies or outside support was not an option we wanted to consider, especially this early into the race. Thankfully, David, Herdip's boyfriend, had given us an emergency igniter as back-up, one that could withstand wet, damp environments, and I couldn't thank him enough. Herdip had met David nine months before the race, and the two had been an item ever since. Amongst all Herdip's suffering out at sea, she was clearly missing David more than anything.

It seemed like everything was particularly difficult for Herdip; even sleeping didn't come easily to her. And in her tired and stressed state she struggled to use the igniter to light the gas stove. It was a rather fiddly piece of equipment, with just a thin rod and a small piece of metal to scrape against it. But every time that Herdip tried to use it she'd either lose precious gas as she failed to get a spark, or burn her fingers with the eventual flame, either of which would cause more stress and frustration. Deciding how much gas to pack for the journey had been a complicated decision as it was. Too little, and we ran the risk of running out. But we didn't want to take too much either: we didn't have much storage space, and an excess of anything wasn't really possible. Even after calculating how much hot water each gas canister heated, and how much hot water we'd need each day for ninety days, all our gas supply had gone missing somewhere in the journey from Newark to La Gomera. We had therefore been forced to rely on the generosity of all the other competitors to share some of their supplies with us, and leaving with less than we had originally intended.

Because of the fire risk from using a gas stove in the cabin, we had fixed a bracket so that the stove could be used out on deck. The bracket meant that the stove rocked with each wave without spilling a drop of our precious water. The process of getting out all the equipment – the stove and gas canister, the kettle, two flasks – setting it all up, lighting it and pouring boiling water from the kettle into the first flask before doing it all again for the second flask – was quite a performance. All this would happen at the rowers' feet – meaning that there was no choice but to carefully observe every single step of the process. This all took time, particularly in the early days when I was adjusting to the routine – extremely precious time, which would otherwise be used to rest, and most importantly, to sleep! But as Herdip struggled to master using the igniter, we were left with no choice other than for me to take over the responsibility of boiling the water, twice a day, every day. On one hand, it was obviously the reasonable thing to do: there was certainly no point in Herdip burning her fingers every time she tried, and we certainly couldn't afford to waste precious gas. But on the other hand I was cursing the fact that I would lose out on 10–15 minutes' break, twice a day, every day, just because that particular task couldn't be shared equally.

Even though I tried really hard to hide my feelings about the unfortunate situation, I found it pretty impossible, and I knew that it would be a contentious issue that would cause an argument before we reached shore.

As the end of our first full week at sea approached I worried about the inevitable discussion of whether we would continue to row on. By now, I was starting to adjust to life on board, and the rowing routine. Most importantly, I was also starting to cope with the sleep deprivation, and I knew that I was more committed than ever to complete the journey. But things didn't seem to be improving for Herdip, and I feared that she would still be keen to leave the boat. I spent all my time at the oars trying to think of a comprehensive argument and reason for staying on the boat, and decided that setting another target to aim for, before giving up, would be the best approach.

> *Two men look through the same bars,*
> *One sees the mud and one the stars ...*
> Anonymous

Following discussions with Pete and Bill from *Gquma Challenger*, we had decided to aim for 20° north and 30° west. After much thought, and acknowledgement of the fact that we didn't have the power to row endless miles in search of the trade winds and favourable currents, we had decided to take a straight line, rather than head south. This was to reduce the number of actual miles that we had to row. As it turned out, we were the only crew that chose that direct straight route, and with hindsight, I appreciate that it impacted on our position in the fleet, especially in those early days.

My new target, therefore, was to persevere until we reached 20° north and 30° west. At that point, it really would show that we had given it a fair go at least, and according to the statistics, those that historically gave up did so within the first week. If we could keep going beyond the first week, I was sure that we could keep going all the way. Thankfully, Herdip agreed. I was a maelstrom of emotion. The relief was intense but I was also very much aware that I was probably being nothing better than a bully in persuading her to stay while she battled so hard.

Even though I was getting used to our new way of life, I still suffered from the physical impact of rowing for twelve hours a day. With three body parts touching the boat at all times – hands, feet, bum – I, like everyone else in the race, was suffering!

Our feet were strapped into foot plates, with the right foot in charge of steering the boat. We were extremely fortunate in that the company Musto had agreed to sponsor us, and had provided our survival suits and some additional technical clothing, including deck shoes. The deck shoes were perfect, not only for giving us a bit of grip when trying to walk on deck, but also when rowing. On hearing the trials and tribulations of the other rowers we were really pleased that we never suffered from as much as one blister on our feet. The only slight niggle would be pain in the right knee from the constant readjusting to the steering.

But if our feet were blister-free, within hours our hands seemed to be one big blister! Even though we'd brought gloves with us for all the crossing, they didn't help. With wave after wave washing over us the gloves were soaking wet straight away. Without the gloves there was at least some hope that our hands could dry out a bit between each wave, which was better for our skin. Within days our blisters had burst and were bleeding into the oars as we rowed, with the sea salt stinging in the wounds. But soon enough a new layer of skin grew over the wounds and we were soon able to hold onto the oars better and row more effectively. Holding on to an oar for twelve hours a day, however, meant that the hands adjust to that position naturally – even when we weren't rowing. Frequently we'd wake up from our break and find our hands cramped into a C shape. Claw hands, as it's called amongst ocean rowers, is one of the side-effects of rowing an ocean, and the pain that shoots up your arms as you try to straighten out each finger is a topic of conversation for hours on end.

There is no comparison between sitting on a comfortable sofa, or a work chair even, and sitting on a small rock-hard rowing seat. Everyone had warned us about the sores from salt chafing, which left the skin on our bums broken, but I suffered much more from what seemed to be pressure sores, which made every inch of bone and muscle in my bum feeling bruised. Since I have such a big bum I'd really hoped that the all the fat would be an extra layer of padding for me! But in reality my weight made it even worse, and early on the deep throbbing pain started to impact on my ability to row as hard as I wanted to for two hours at a time. I'd often had to perform a little bum-dance to cope with the pain – left cheek up, row, right cheek up, row, both cheeks, row.

The thing that caused the most unbearable pain of all, however, was the oars banging against my shins. Frequently a wave would throw *Dream Maker* up in the air, and seconds later we'd land on the next wave, usually at an awkward angle. If leaning to one side the oar on that side would hit the water first, ripping that oar from our grip. It happened so quickly and so forcefully that I could do nothing to stop the oar from crashing down onto my shins – with the whole weight of the boat travelling through it. It would happen time and time again within a two-hour rowing shift, and more often than not, it would land on the exact same spot. My shins were covered in bruises and the pain would shoot through me unlike anything I'd ever felt before. For a brief second I'd lose control of all my senses and scream out in pain, while big tears would sting my eyes.

I just couldn't think of anything to stop it from happening, and I longed for my shin pads from my rugby kit bag back in London. We'd already lowered our seats on the deck in the hope that it would help slightly. Occasionally I was able to squeeze my thumb between the oar and my shin to cushion the blow. Herdip managed to do that more often than I did and we finally realised that Herdip's fingers were all nearly half an inch longer than mine. When holding the oars her thumb and index finger would overlap. My hands were so small that there was a big gap between my thumb and index finger. It's amazing what you notice when you have nothing other than rowing to do for twenty-four hours!

Nearly two weeks into the race a full moon finally appeared in the night sky. Without any clouds to block its light we were finally able to enjoy the experience of rowing on a calm sea with the moon reflecting on the waves like a silver carpet – directing the way. With a gentle breeze and rolling waves travelling with us the rowing was enjoyable and we could spot the reflection of a bright star or two dancing on the waves. It truly felt like paradise for me at those moments, and I couldn't help but be amazed at the vast enormity of the universe and how insignificantly small we humans are.

The lighter nights made us more aware of the large number of fish swimming around us at night. They were brightly-coloured fish of all sizes and would stay with us for hours – probably using us to protect themselves from the predatory fish! It was the flying fish that gave us most amusement – and most grief. I'd gaze in amazement as I witnessed them flying through the air from wave to wave, travelling some considerable distance, while their beautifully bright-coloured skin shone in the sun. But the smaller ones, and probably less experienced, would not be as elegant performing their tricks and they'd end up crashing into us on their way to the next waves. At night, possibly distracted by our deck light, they would crash more frequently. But no matter how many times it happened it would always give me a mini heart attack as another wet fish crashed onto the deck and banged its wings around frantically. While dreaming away in the darkness of the night, it was a particularly distressing experience to be slapped across the face by one! Unfortunately it was very few that we were able to rescue and return to the sea in time. Getting hold of their wet slimy skin and holding their moving wings was often impossible. Some of the smaller ones would land without us noticing and it was only a few days later that a rotten smell would tell us that we had company on the deck!

As we approached two weeks at sea, it seemed that things were getting no easier for poor Herdip. Just as the seasickness and nausea finally started to ease and she finally began to be able to eat, another misfortune came her way.

Our daily menu for the trip included three freeze-dried meals. We were using standard army-ration-type packs, which are often used by adventurers and expeditions as they last for years, are high in calories, and are easy to prepare. All that needs to be done is to pour boiling water over the contents and leave to stand for around ten minutes. We had ordered most of our meals from the British company Expedition Foods and all packs were in a bright orange foil bag with a little sticker on it announcing the apparent content.

Twice daily I'd get out the gas cooker and boil enough water to last for both of us for the day, then we'd pour it into flasks to keep it hot. It was while pouring the hot water from the flask into one of the orange foil packs that Herdip was caught off guard by a wave, spilling the hot water and scalding her leg and foot. Given the sea state it's a common problem, and it is a surprise that it didn't happen more often, to be honest, but it was a tough blow for Herdip, who was already suffering enough. I tended to the wounds with cream and dressings, and although it wouldn't win any badges from St John's Ambulance for appearance it did the job; it was the best I could do in the cramped moving cabin with both of us in there. Luckily, Herdip's burns didn't stop her from being able to row, and we could continue with our shift rota.

Nearly three weeks in I decided to go back into the water to clean the hull. As we rowed so slowly, no faster than 2.5 knots mostly, the barnacles had a field day attaching themselves to us. They'd grown an inch and more despite the coat of anti-foul that we'd applied on the hull before leaving. The belief amongst the experienced rowers is that they slow the progress considerably over time. So armed with snorkelling goggles and a paint scraper I jumped back into the big blue and set to work. It wasn't a calm day, and probably far from sensible to be holding my breath under the hull as the boat bounced up and down on top of my head. But there was nothing really sensible about our adventure and the psychological benefit of thinking that it made an improvement to our rowing speed made the effort seem worthwhile.

If facing life at sea without hot water would be a challenging obstacle to our chances of completing the row, being without any drinking water would have certainly put an end to our dreams. On the morning of December 18, my godson Rhun's birthday, we were facing such a predicament.

As per race rules, every pair's boat carries 150 litres of water bottles as ballast at the bottom of the boat. In the worst case scenario, if the boat was to capsize, it is designed to self-correct and pop back round with the help of the heavy ballasts. The water was also there for cases of emergency if we were to face water shortage, but if the seal of more than four litres of water was broken Woodvale would add a time penalty during scrutineering after arriving back on land – a penalty which increased with every additional litre of water broken. This is primarily done to stop the super-competitive crews from being tempted to lighten the load on the boat to increase their rowing speed, but no one wants to risk the penalty time. Despite actually arriving in Antigua first, James Cracknell and Ben Fogle were awarded second place in the race rankings back in 2007 because they had to use their ballast water for drinking.

It would have been impossible to carry enough water supplies for the duration of the trip anyway, and we were completely reliant on our SPECTRA water-maker. This piece of equipment is one of the wonders of modern technology, and through relying on the power generated by our solar panels the water-maker can convert 20 litres of sea water into drinking water in an hour. Every morning, as soon as we had a bit of sun shining on the solar panels, we'd switch on the water-maker to provide us with our water supply for that day. The machine made a familiar humming noise in the bottom of the boat somewhere, and even though we couldn't see it, just hearing the noise was enough to inform us that all was in working order. Indeed we named the noise our on-board gremlin. But that morning it was a very different gremlin that we heard grunting in the background, and without a drop of water appearing through the pipe we knew we had a problem. A big problem! I went into a state of panic! We carried a hand pump on board as well, but the idea of hand-pumping every single drop of water needed for two to three hours a day during my break time certainly did not appeal! Being so reliant on a single piece of equipment to allow us to stay in the race was worrying. Yet, in the back of my mind, I couldn't help but think that retiring from the race because of equipment failure seemed so much better than dropping out just because we couldn't cope with the hardship of the challenge.

We carried the manual on board, but after much inspecting we were making no progress. Thankfully we also had the telephone number of the water-maker specialist back in the UK, who had actually serviced ours just before departure. Following a phone call to him, via the satellite phone, the hope was that the problem was caused by an airlock in the system. If the sea state is rough when using the water-maker the risk is that air, not water, is sucked up into the system, causing a block. After much exploring, and untangling of pipe after pipe the SPECTRA was working again. It was certainly a bitter-sweet relief.

4

Day after day

He who moves not forward goes backward.
Johann Wolfgang von Goethe

Anyone can hold the helm when the sea is calm.
Publius Syrus (c.42 BC) Maxim, 358

Time, and my perception of time, became one big confused state in which I couldn't figure out what had happened when. On one level every second stood still for an eternity, and on another level three weeks had passed in the blink of an eye. We'd already experienced so much, but yet we were miles away from completing our challenge, and everything was blurring into one messy state.

My three weeks on the Atlantic Ocean, and the three weeks' countdown towards Christmas that my friends and family were experiencing back home, could not have been more different. Christmas had never been so meaningful and meaningless before.

Christmas Eve was miserable, with a strong gale blowing large waves across our beam, leaving us bitterly cold and fearful for our safety. Given the low mood on deck we decided to hatch up for the night, and let *Dream Maker* take its own course wherever that may be. When we woke up on Christmas morning, therefore, our first consideration was our position. Thankfully we had travelled six miles towards Antigua, which was as good as a gift as any that day. But I just couldn't avoid that gnawing feeling that I was missing out on a fun-filled day back home with all my family. The longing for home is all the more intense at Christmas, and the *hiraeth* that day certainly made me appreciate once more how blessed I'd been in my upbringing.

Herdip and I wore Santa hats and earrings in the shape of a snowman and a Christmas tree to give a Christmassy feel to the day. Herdip gave me a beautiful bracelet. I opened the gifts that friends and family had kindly given me before I left, and I prepared for a live interview on Radio Wales. I can't remember a word of what I talked about with the presenter that day, but I'll never forget the pre-recorded messages that my parents had sent for me to hear, and the tuneful carol being sang by all the local children in Parc. Sadly the satellite phone wasn't so appreciative of the Christmas carol being sung and we lost the signal, cutting the interview short halfway though the singing. It was a bitter reminder of those days in Lesotho, but a saving grace that stopped all of Wales hearing me cry live on the radio.

Herdip and I took a break from the rowing together around lunchtime to mark our unique Christmas experience, and we celebrated with a small piece of Christmas cake from Marks & Spencer. I got to devour all of the marzipan while Herdip got to enjoy the icing. It was certainly a great contrast to my usual Christmas day excess.

Although Father Christmas hadn't been man enough to find us out there amongst the waves, we were treated to a far more useful visitor that day. The race support yacht *Kilcullen* came to visit. Since that first horrific night, over three weeks previously we hadn't seen another soul (not counting the soldier that Herdip saw sitting on the oar!). *Kilcullen* was crewed by three lively men, and their colourful characters would beam across the waves as they sailed skilfully around us. To find us out there amongst the waves must have been as hard as finding a needle in a haystack, and I could only beam a smile from ear to ear as I spotted the white sail appearing on the horizon, and heard their deep voices shouting festive greetings – even if they did taunt us slightly, sipping their cans of cold beers on deck.

But as enjoyable as their company was, their visit had a more important reason than merely popping by to share some seasonal greetings. Our ARGOS tracking beacon, another one of our essential pieces of equipment, wasn't working. It is through this piece of equipment and the satellite dishes in the sky that Woodvale, the race organisers, kept an eye on all the boats in the race, twenty-four hours a day – each boat's position, speed and direction of travel. Important information if a rescue mission was ever needed.

Just as important as our safety, of course, it was also the piece of kit that was connected to the race website which allowed all the supporters at home to track our progress. Every boat was represented by a differently coloured dot, and that dot would extend like a snake across the computer screen as we moved across the ocean. Our colour was a pale blue, and that dot became the lifeline for friends and family at home to follow us while we were out at sea. Every six hours our position was updated on the website, and this was the only way that our supporters could have an insight into our true situation. In bad weather, when we couldn't row, the dot would turn on itself in circles on the screen. Although this gave everyone a clear indication of what we were experiencing at that time, it also caused a lot of worry and concern about our well-being.

But on that Christmas day there was no chance of sleeping off the excess of a turkey dinner. With instructions from Jim over the radio I followed each and every single wire from the ARGOS across the deck and into the power supply and back a thousand times over, checking each connection and finally changing the fuse box to get it working again.

The visit and the worry over the ARGOS was a godsend, and before we knew it Christmas day was nearly over without too many tears. The visit from *Kilcullen* certainly rated as one of the best Christmas gifts I'd ever had, but on Boxing Day there was no escaping the fact that we were making no progress. Strong winds from the east prevented us from taking the southerly course that we wanted, and stopped us from reaching our all-important way-point of 20° north 30° west.

In desperation I stupidly jumped off deck and back into the rough sea again to scrape away at any stubborn barnacles that may have been hindering our progress. But even more stupidly I came up with a plan! It was clear to me by that point that the real reason for our slow progress was because our boat was too heavy, and the only solution was to make it lighter! The only obvious way that we could make it lighter would be to throw some of our large stock of freeze-dried food over board. The race rules stated that we had to have enough food supply to be out at sea for ninety days. Ninety days! Did I really intend to be out at sea for ninety days? Never! So I insisted that Herdip and I hand-pick our favourite food packs to last for another forty-five days. It was quite some ceremony as we cast it all overboard, pack after pack, and we laughed at the thought of tens of fish feasting on it for years to come. Obviously, however, it made no difference to our travelling speed, and I was soon to regret my stupid decision.

After some thought and discussion we decided to abandon our fight to reach 20° north 30° west, and to travel instead with the wind in the general direction of Antigua, despite the overwhelming psychological need to reach 20°

north. A more experienced crew would probably have made that decision days earlier, especially considering that we had over 1,800 miles left to push south. But having set 20° north 30° west as a waypoint, and our next target to aim for, it was emotionally really difficult not to be able to achieve it.

The days continued to pass at a more rapid pace than the miles did, and soon it was time to wave goodbye to 2007. I'll never forget where I was to welcome in 2008.

In a storm a few days previously our VHF aerial had snapped off at its base. Luckily we'd managed to save it from being washed out to sea, but we didn't have a clue about how to fix it back on. Without an aerial our VHF seemed pretty much useless. At the crest of a wave we had a chance of being able to make contact with ships that were up to fifteen miles away. Without an aerial, we had no idea what distance we could reach, if at all.

As the sun set, leaving its usual array of beautiful colours dancing on the waves, a large tanker ship appeared on the horizon. Once again it appeared that it was heading directly for us, and once again I started to be consumed by fear. Without a VHF radio that we could rely on I was certain that we were in even more imminent danger. I reached for the grab bag, which contained an additional hand-held VHF radio as a back-up, and stood on the deck, peering towards the horizon for a clue on the ship's direction of travel. Instinctively I started to talk to Herdip in the cabin by using the hand-held radio. The original idea was to see if the VHF had any signal at all, but getting somewhat carried away with the emotion of the moment I started to describe in detail the scene that was unfolding in front of me. As the ship got closer my description got more detailed and more explicit. Herdip responded dramatically to my commentary and both of us broke every maritime rule on the proper way of communicating at sea! After some stupid sentence along the line of 'Big ship, big ship, can you hear us? This is a very little rowing boat and you're about to crash over us and make us fish food', I nearly fell overboard in shock when a deep voice with a French accent answered over the air waves, 'Yes, I can hear you very well, what is your position?' Herdip's uncontrollable laughter burst out of the cabin and I could hardly concentrate on our longitude and latitude to relay back the numbers, such was my embarrassment. The deep invisible voice sounded very attractive, but he clearly had no interest in making small talk with us, or even in wishing us a 'Bonne année'. Most unlike the French to be curt, I thought!

The plan for welcoming in 2008 was to take a break from the rowing just before midnight so that we could both savour the moment, and celebrate with a cup of hot chocolate and let off a flare into the night's sky to mark the occasion. But as the countdown for midnight actually approached I actually sat by myself out on deck imagining the chimes of Big Ben announcing the arrival of a new year. What I could actually hear was Herdip on the satellite phone with David, her boyfriend, close to tears once more. The cabin walls were so thin that not one phone conversation could be private. I said a small prayer, asking for a healthy and happy new year for all my friends and family at home, and that we could land safely, and soon! I looked around, absorbing the elation of being out there; savouring all the phosphorescence that burst into life as if they were reflecting the stars sparkling in the night's sky, while the moon was reflected on the rolling waves that gently rose and fell around us. I knew then that the ocean had me captured.

After I returned from the crossing I was often asked if I ever felt lonely while out there. I missed my close friends and family: of course. The Welsh *hiraeth*: yes. Self-pity: for sure. But loneliness, no. I don't ever remember feeling lonely out there. Being alone is not the same as being lonely, of course. And even though I was hundreds and hundreds of miles away from civilisation all the messages of support that we received daily made me feel that the whole of the world were travelling with us. All the messages were like some sort of comfort blanket, hugging us closely as we crossed the waves. And I often asked myself, how can I expect anyone else to enjoy my company if I can't enjoy it myself? For me, not being able to relate to the people around you on an emotional level is what constitutes real loneliness. And later on, while I struggled to re-adjust to life back on land, I experienced the real heartache of loneliness while surrounded by lots of people.

As the days turned into weeks we finally established a pretty efficient routine. Every chore, however, seemed to take a lot of effort and energy. Everything took so much more time to complete than it would do on land. Time was one of our most valuable commodities, which I desperately tried to save for the real important task of sleeping! Personal hygiene was one chore that was often sacrificed in order to catch a few more minute's sleep. At best, a weekly shower and a daily brush of our teeth was all that I did! It was only during those few precious minutes while brushing our teeth in the galley that we ever stood up – fully weight-bearing on both feet! And after the first week or so we used it as an opportunity to show off our new found sea legs! Considering that there isn't much opportunity to stand up out there, we were left to watch our leg muscles slowly waste away. Getting across the deck to use the 'ladies' (a big, red, uncomfortable, bucket) was challenging enough on all fours, let alone by trying to walk it. There was no alternative other than to accept that we'd land in Antigua with bendy chicken legs to complement our broad shoulders!

Our poor personal hygiene habits eventually also extended to our eating habits. As spoon after spoon snapped, we were left with just one spoon between us. Neither of us could be bothered with the effort required to wash up even one piece of utensil, so there was no option other than to lick the spoon clean after every meal, ready for the other to use. As Herdip is a vegetarian I had to be extra diligent after a meal containing meat, and lick a few times more!

A few days into the New Year we finally managed to reach below 20 degrees north. But far from being welcomed by any favourable winds or currents, once again the weather was unfavourable. Because of the strong wind the sea state was rough, and waves well over 30 feet would frequently crash over us. After one particularly brutal wave crashed over us we decided to sit it out on the para-anchor once more. Even on the para-anchor we were being battered, and after eight hours we'd been blown back what it had taken us 30 hours to row. It's impossible to explain in words the emotion that rages inside as you watch the GPS slowly moving back over old ground, as it were. Depressing doesn't quite seem to give the emotion justice. And while sitting in that small cabin, being thrown from side to side, just like a sock in a washing machine, there is absolutely nothing that can be done about it! To make the situation even more unbearable we'd been without sun for days, and our power supply was dangerously low. As we hardly had enough power for the water-maker we couldn't kill the time writing messages home, listening to music or reading even – we had no power for any such luxuries. With both of us in the cabin, even resting comfortably was beyond question. The cabin was too small to sit up in, and whenever one of us needed to move position the other had to move as well. With each wave that smashed into us forcefully, one of us would crash on top of the other – which was always a particular challenge when poor Herdip ended up at the bottom! The only way that we could try to jam ourselves into position was for us both to face the same direction and for Herdip to press her knees into my back. It was hardly comfortable, but at least it saved her from being squashed!

After five weeks at sea every minute once again seemed like a real battle. Five day passed with no sun to shine on our solar panels. Our power supply was now so low that even our ARGOS tracking beacon couldn't transmit a signal.

To make sure that we were coping in the rough conditions *Kilcullen* came to visit us once more. This time, however, because of the size of the waves they couldn't come so close, or stay for long. They quickly gave us a few words of advice on how to fix the VHF aerial, which was actually transmitting for a distance of only just over a mile. We'd been very close to that Frenchman on New Year's Eve!

I struggled with equipment that I'd never used before to do the repairs in the short time we had before *Kilcullen* disappeared over the horizon again, and was hugely relieved when the aerial was finally reattached to the cabin roof and transmitting for a radius of around eight miles. When it came down to it, it was a strip of duct tape that saved the day, and I couldn't believe that we were so reliant on something so simple. Like one of our supporters said, 'Duct tape is like the force. It has a dark side, a light side, and it holds the universe together'. It was certainly holding our world together!

Shortly before *Kilcullen* came to see us two dolphins swam by us. They hadn't stayed for long, despite our excitement at seeing them. But shortly after *Kilcullen* left around *ten* dolphins came to swim around us. To watch them was mesmerising, and it felt like the two we had seen earlier in the day had said, 'Come on boys, let's go back to see those two girls – they looked like they could do with some help!' And finally, the following day we had some sun.

Dreams make the impossible possible;
Dedication makes the possible probable;
And work makes the probable happen.
Jim Trefethen

If the wind will not serve, take the oars.
Dihareb Ladin

With so much misfortune happening to Herdip I became really worried about how long she could stay on the boat. Even though she agreed on one level to stay her spirits were not improving at all as the days went past, and she really seemed to be going through a personal hell. As I came out on deck to start my shift at the oars the first thing that would greet me would be Herdip in tears. Sometimes it would feel as if she cried continuously, and pretty soon I just didn't know how or what I could possibly do to comfort her. I tried in all the ways that I could think of, said all the encouraging words I could muster, but yet it was not enough. So after a while I chose to ignore the tears completely. She longed to be back at home, and would ask over and over again, 'When do you think we'll arrive?' Despite thinking pretty much of nothing else, counting the miles per hour, to calculate the miles per day so that I could divide it with the distance left to estimate our arrival date – in truth, just like everyone else – I had no idea when that would be. Yes, we could row as hard as we could, but our arrival date was ultimately determined by the weather.

It seemed that there was nothing I could do to help Herdip and the situation was slowly ebbing away at my spirits too. I wanted to scream, to pull my hair out by the roots. At times I longed to call the race organisers to ask them to collect her so that she could escape from this hell that she was experiencing and so that I could be left to enjoy the rest of the crossing on my own. I knew that continuing on my own would be hard and that the worry for my parents would be a thousand times more, but at times I felt utterly convinced that anything would be better than spending twenty-four hours a day, for an endless amount of days and weeks, in the company of someone who was so sad.

I'm sure that the way I was enjoying it out there so much was irritating Herdip, as much as the fact that she was so unhappy was tiring me. I wrote in a blog entry one day: 'I can't believe how much I love it out here. I am battered and bruised and physically exhausted but love it so much all the same'. It was impossible to comprehend how two people could share the exact same experience and respond to it all so differently. Was it because my company was so unbearable? Was I really bullying her unfairly to stay? I was completely guilt-ridden as I quietly wished that she would leave the boat, while at the same time continuously praying that she would stay. Whatever our current situation, our current differences, I knew that she was a crucial part of the campaign and that she had exactly the same right to succeed as I did. Given how much she hated the experience, she probably deserved it even more.

Although every second of rowing seemed painful, being forced to rest in the cabin during a storm was no more pleasurable. To go from rowing twelve hours a day to lying in the same position for hours on end while our bodies seized up made every fibre in our bodies scream in pain. To add to our misery, while caged in the cabin because of unfavourable winds, receiving a race update telling us that another boat in the fleet had gone past us was crushing. After years of playing rugby I couldn't be anything but competitive. Falling to the back of the fleet hurt. On one level I could rationalise perfectly well that worrying about race positions while battling with all the elements was futile, foolish even. But I just couldn't press a 'mute' button to silence the competitive voice screaming in the back of my mind.

And this was yet another issue to cause tension between Herdip and me. I was completely reliant on the daily race update on the fleet. And although Herdip studied them with me, she probably hated the effect that it had on me. In trying to explain the situation in a blog one day I could only summarise the difference in our objectives as 'completing' and 'competing'. For Herdip it was all about 'completing' – as quickly as possible. But I longed to 'compete', to stay in the race until the last minute, and as much as it hurt, I still insisted on getting the race updates, despite the painful realisation that we were falling to the back of the fleet. Finally, and probably too late, I realised that I couldn't 'compete' on my own.

In reality, competing against the elements is what each and every one of us was doing; some just had more power and luck with the weather to deal with it. But then we received a message from Jo Bardoe, Mia's mum, saying, 'It must be so frustrating to be reliant on the elements and nature. I guess that ties in nicely with what you are doing. The money you raise will go towards making important changes to people's lives and NOT allowing nature to take its unfortunate course with some of the children with metabolic conditions'. Our self-imposed challenge was nothing compared to the daily challenge that Mia, and children like Mia, face every day. Theirs is an important battle. Our position in the race didn't even come close to registering.

It was the messages of support and encouragement we received that kept us going across the waves; there is no doubt about that. We were receiving tens of messages daily and from fifteen countries across the world, often from people that we didn't even know. Although I couldn't believe it, or comprehend it, according to the messages we were inspiring others to go and achieve their own dreams. By then, it seemed that we were rowing on behalf of each and every one of our supporters. Our efforts gave others the boost to battle their own challenges. Our dream was to row across the Atlantic Ocean, but a lot of other dreams were being inspired on the way.

5

The daily grind

Impossible is just a big word thrown around by small men
who find it easier to live in the world they've been given
than to explore the power they have to change it.
Impossible is not a fact. It's an opinion.
It's not a declaration. It's a dare.
Impossible is potential.
Impossible is temporary.
Impossible is nothing.
Muhammad Ali

Dream big and dare to fail.
Norman Vaughan

Wearing wet clothes isn't particularly pleasurable at any time. Heavy rain, a wild wave, sweat or condensation – the cause doesn't change the outcome – it's miserable. Very early on we didn't have one item of dry clothing. We couldn't even keep our sleeping bag or the toilet paper dry!

Despite the miserable weather that battered us for most of the first few weeks in January there was one aspect that I just couldn't stop enjoying. I welcomed the numerous rainbows that appeared in the sky with sheer delight. They were large and bright, with every single one of the colours clearly seen as it reached from one end of the horizon to the other. Occasionally, on a calm day the colours would reflect on the sea as well. Apart from being a sign that favourable weather might be on its way, to see nature at its best like that was a huge boost to my morale. Amongst the shades of blue and grey that surrounded us continuously there was a distinct lack of colour to invigorate our senses. There was no vibrant green of Welsh hills and mountains in the distance, or a bright yellow daffodil to brighten up our cabin. So to gaze at a rainbow was a real pleasure, and even though the camera never did justice to the scene that we were seeing I took dozens of photos so that I would never forget that beauty.

As we got closer to Antigua, we were once again crossing the shipping lanes, and seeing ships and tankers on the horizon more frequently. Some of the competitors were also, by now, reaching land. Our friends on *Pura Vida* had stormed in first, and the battle for the first pair's boat to arrive had been a particularly hard-fought contest between *Gquma Challenge* and *No Fear*. Delighted as we were with their success, and inspired by knowing it could be done and that there really was land over the horizon, I could not but feel a hint of envy, knowing that we were so far back in the fleet with so far left to row.

But when the time came for the GPS to declare that we only had 999 miles left between us and Antigua, a huge storm had broken on *Dream Maker*, and there was no celebration. After eight weeks of being together, without so much as spending a second apart, attempting minute after minute to avoid saying or doing anything that may break the peace – the first fight broke out between Herdip and me.

Herdip had been unable to steer by using the GPS alone. The battery in the compass had died in the first few days, and after eight weeks of shining some light on it our head torch had also died. It had been my responsibility to order and pack spare batteries, and Herdip was furious that I hadn't packed any for the compass. I was equally annoyed that we hadn't installed a compass with light generated from the solar panel rather than on battery, but there was no denying I had messed up. After one particularly dark and miserable night, rowing without knowing for certain that she was steering on the right course, Herdip lost it. Unfortunately for us both I decided to use the occasion to voice my opinion about her contribution to the campaign in general. Everything came out in one wild stream of accusations, every complaint, every annoyance, every frustration, until there was nothing left to say. The silence that followed was unbearable. Neither of us uttered a word for hours as both of us blamed the other for everything that was unbearable about the crossing.

I sat in the cabin raging, and nastily eating Herdip's share of chocolate to try and make some sort of point! The wind changed and I knew that there was a squall heading our way. Within minutes the rain came, and the noise as each drop crashed against the cabin roof was deafening. I knew that Herdip's skin would probably be stinging by now as each heavy rain drops were hurled at her with force, and that pretty soon she would be freezing cold from being so wet. Since the first week Herdip had been using my waterproof jacket because the lightweight one she'd bought with her was not waterproof. Swapping over at the end of a shift had become a challenging business as we tried to swap over the jacket out on deck quickly, while praying that a wave wouldn't hit us at that exact moment – soaking the one that was about to start her break. But following our fight that night I was too reluctant to offer her my jacket and she was probably too proud to ask. I listened to every rain drop crash on the cabin roof, consumed with feelings of guilt, rage, shame and resentment – all of them blurring into each other. Thankfully the rain washed away the atmosphere and finally some sun and chatting appeared once more.

At times I just couldn't help but feel that the elements really were trying at every opportunity to kill our dream. Our pathetic efforts at rowing against it were useless. We had no option other than to sit and wait patiently for a moment of opportunity and so give it our all then. There was no point in wasting our energy and emotion battling it. Shouting or screaming or losing my temper would make not one ounce of difference. I promised then that I would never let the small irritations of land annoy me on my return. Nothing could possibly be as frustrating as yielding every ounce of control and relying completely on the elements of the ocean while sitting in a tiny rowing boat. After all, it's always going to be the Atlantic Ocean that wins. We could never conquer the Atlantic Ocean in a rowing boat; we could just pray for the opportunity to pass through.

> *The next time your life flashes before your eyes,*
> *Make sure you have something worth watching.*
> Anon

> *It doesn't have to be fun to be fun.*
> Mark Twight

January was quickly disappearing, and the realisation that we were going to be out at sea much longer than we had thought was slowly sinking in, let alone that we were now rapidly running out of food! The last week of January was particularly difficult for me, and for a while I was in a pretty grumpy state. That week Steve, my ex-husband, was flying out to Thailand to get married. Steve had come to meet me at Gatwick airport for a final goodbye before I flew out to La Gomera, and had told me then that he would remarry while

I was out at sea. I was the one that had brought our relationship to an end, and even though it hadn't been an easy decision I certainly had no right to feel bitter about things now. But while sitting there on *Dream Maker*, imagining them on a paradise island getting married while I was wet, smelly, with salt sores and boils on my ass, I couldn't help but feel sorry for myself. I wallowed in self-pity and allowed the tears to flow. Herdip tried her best to console me, with our roles now reversed, and she even gave me all the ginger jelly men from the Haribo sweet bag – my absolute favourite. But nothing worked.

So just like all other times when I feel sad there was nothing I could do other than phone Mam! Yes, my poor Mam! What exactly did I expect her to say to make things better, while sitting at home thousands of miles away, I don't know. But I knew that just hearing her voice would somehow ease some of the heartache.

It was a completely different type of pain that I experienced the following day. By now we were sharing one pair of Musto deck shoes to give the other pair a chance to dry out. Sadly that meant that we didn't have any grip while moving around on the deck in bare feet. I was just climbing out of the cabin, with one foot either side of the hatch, when a rogue wave crashed against us, throwing me completely off balance. I fell awkwardly, landing with my coccyx on the hatch hinge. The pain was excruciating and I was sure that I would never ever be able to sit down again – not much comfort, as I had to get on with rowing while sitting down if I was ever to get out of there.

The weather was highly variable, changing from one minute to the next. A scorching sun would be replaced by large grey clouds and heavy rain in seconds. The wind had a mind of its own, and once again we were going round and round in circles while sitting on the para-anchor.

Once again cramped in the cabin on a dark and miserable night we didn't have any enthusiasm for anything, so when the Sea-Me started to bleep it just seemed that it was just one more annoyance to our night. The obvious temptation was just to ignore it, especially as it had been bleeping sporadically for no apparent reason over the last few weeks. But with both of us confined to the cabin it seemed more dangerous than ever without someone keeping an eye out on the horizon, so now and again I'd force myself to open the hatch door and peer out into the darkness – praying each time that I wouldn't be soaked with a passing wave at that precise moment. It was a particularly dark night, with no moon and a heavy low cloud, and each time I peered out I knew it would be tough to spot any ships or tankers out there. With the Sea-Me bleeping louder and more frequently I forced myself to look out into the darkness once again. But as all I could see was one bright star in the distance, I quickly retreated back into the cabin to rest. But the Sea-Me had other ideas and began to screech out in one loud continous bleep which forced me to stumble out on to the deck to look properly. I just couldn't believe my own eyes as the star that I'd previously seen was actually a bright light on top of a mast – within a few meters and heading straight towards us. I screamed in sheer panic and thankfully the yacht was crewed rather than on auto-pilot. Whoever was at the helm must have heard my scream and changed their course instantaneously – we had very narrowly avoided a collision. Although it was probably only about a forty-foot yacht it would have been more than enough to rip straight through us. There but for the grace of God ...

People are about as happy
as they decide that they are going to be.
Abraham Lincoln

The rugby Six Nations clashes started and were a reminder, if one was needed, that life at home was moving on without us. Since 1999, when I'd started playing rugby in the Wales 'A' squad, I hadn't missed following the championships. Luckily there were plenty of volunteers at hand to send me live commentaries of the games, and the Woodvale message board was flowing with banter between the Welsh and English supporters that were following our progress too.

The day that Wales beat England was momentous for more than one reason. Herdip was rowing while I was on edge in the cabin getting regular updates on the satellite phone as each point was scored. At the same second that the final message came through to say that Wales had won, a huge wave crashed against us, throwing Herdip off her seat. Thankfully she was unharmed – and in the midst of it all she came up with a genius idea! Detach the LED light that was fixed in the bow cabin and rewire it across the deck to attach it to the compass. She worked away at it during her break and was bursting with pride as her idea took shape. She beamed as she rowed that night, with a bright LED light shining the way. It was a tremendous boost for her in more than one way, and her spirits rose considerably.

The days were all now blurring into one, and the weeks were racing past. Karen and Duncan were preparing to fly out to Antigua to be there to greet me as we landed! Karen is the most amazing loyal friend, and shortly after I'd announced my ambition she had supported me every step of the way, just as she had supported me during the dark days of my divorce. To mark her confidence in my ability to complete the crossing she had booked her flight to Antigua for the dates that we had planned to land – between sixty and seventy days after departure. But it was obvious by now that we wouldn't reach land in that time, and that Karen would be flying back home while we still had hundreds of miles left to row. But they had to go out there anyway, and not only to enjoy a relaxing holiday: I had nothing to wear on my arrival, and so was completely reliant on Karen flying over to bring my things! During the planning and preparation I hadn't discussed once with my parents about the possibility of them flying out to Antigua to see me land. I didn't want to put any pressure on them, and knew that flying so far for a holiday was far from being their ideal choice. Even though it would be a memorable occasion for me, I knew it wasn't fair to pressurise them to being there. I should never have doubted that they would be there, though. Soon into the crossing Dad announced that he was looking forward to an unusual holiday before lambing season started that year!

The emotional aspect that I struggled with the most was the fact that I would miss out on key events that I had been looking forward to, because the crossing was taking longer than we had planned. It had been a big mistake to set certain dates to which I could look forward. For example, I'd planned to enjoy relaxing on the golden beaches of Antigua with Karen before flying out to Las Vegas to present the results of my research in a conference, and then head home to get all dressed up for a St Valentine's ball, which Jo Bardoe had arranged to raise money for our campaign and the Gaucher Association. By now I had to accept that I would miss out on all of those.

I was familiar with missing out on exciting events in a quest to fulfil a sporting dream. For years I had sacrificed dinner-dates with my friends for club rugby training, city weekend breaks for Welsh rugby training, and holidays in the sun with my friends for rugby tours and Six Nations matches. It was a choice that I was happy to make in my mission to be fully capped for my country. In the end it was never to be. My rugby career seemed a bitter-sweet combination of failure and success. I was successful in gaining thirteen Welsh 'A' caps but failed in getting the all-important full cap. But despite the sacrifices I will never regret my time in my rugby boots.

On one level, rowing an ocean is easier than getting selected to play rugby for your country. In rugby you're reliant on others – the preferred game-style of the coaches and the performances of the other players competing for your position. To row across an ocean it's just down to you get into a boat and row ...

With every hope of crossing within seventy days now gone I was left regretting my stupid decision of throwing all that food overboard on Boxing Day, merely three weeks into our crossing. Tasting the same food, meal after meal, day after day, was now incredibly tedious, and our chocolate supply had finished weeks ago. By then, recycling a tea bag three or four times a day was the biggest pleasure we had on board. We were also running dangerously low on toilet paper, and nobody wanted to imagine the consequences of that!

With five hundred miles to go I rationalised that if we needed to be rescued, the Antigua and Barbados Sea Rescue should find us within twenty-four hours. I figured that I could last for twenty-four hours in a life-raft without chocolate so I raided the emergency grab bag for the emergency ration of chocolate. My need for chocolate was just too great to resist any further. You can never overexaggerate how much pleasure a girl can have from indulging on a bar of chocolate.

After spending the first weeks battling to push south we were spending the last few weeks battling from being pushed too far south. We were worried that if we approached Antigua from too southerly a position we wouldn't be able to hit the finishing line, given the strength of the tide there. We knew we had to be particularly careful with our bearings – especially without Frank and his boat there to rescue us. But the wind was adamant that it would confuse things for us. Regardless of our efforts we just couldn't maintain a consistent daily mileage in the direction we wanted, and although we were closely approaching Antigua the end just never seemed to be in sight.

6

Landing in Antigua

In the confrontation between the stream and the rock,
the stream always wins,
though not through strength but by perseverance.
H. Jackson Brown

The last few hours were as unbearable as the first few, although those emotions seemed to be from a different era now. I was suffering badly with toothache and the combination of antibiotics and painkillers had played havoc with my stomach. The emotions of the moment were most likely contributing to the chaos. We were about to reach the end of our crossing.

The lights of Shirley Heights on the corner of Antigua had been visible on the horizon for some hours, and the regular blinking was hypnotic to watch. We'd experienced a calm night, and had slept with the hatch door open. I gazed at the stars, which appeared so bright in the night sky, their reflection dancing lively on the waves. I made myself notice every single detail to record a vivid image in my mind, one that would always remind me of the magical feeling of being there. It was an experience so serene that I never wanted to forget.

We were drifting gently on a bearing of 270 degrees towards the finishing line, an invisible line that was crucial within the race rules. We had to cross that exact line to have an official ranking in the race. After eleven weeks at sea, wondering and worrying if we'd ever get close to it, we were now so close that we could practically have swum to it.

I gazed up to the sky once more. I knew that somewhere up there my Mam, Dad and my sister Gles were flying over to see me land. That was the reason that we had been sitting drifting, not rowing a stroke for three days. After spending every single minute of the crossing estimating our arrival date, with the predicted dates changing daily, if not hourly, deciding when the three should fly out to meet us had been a tricky process. The bitter disappointment of missing Karen and Duncan played so heavily on my mind that I didn't want to risk a repeat situation. But pretty much immediately after booking the flight the weather changed, and all of a sudden we were blown towards Antigua at a rapid rate.

Pretty quickly we all realised the obvious – rather than my family standing at the finish to see their daughter rowing triumphantly to the shore, Herdip and I would have landed before they did, and I would be at the airport waiting for my family! There was nothing that could be done, therefore, other than to stop rowing! But even then, we drifted with the wind and the currents at such a rapid pace that we still feared that we would land before them. Any delay on the flight and we'd have a major problem with the timing. After all the emotions, all the worry, all the experiences, they just *had* to be there to share the celebration, and the relief of seeing us reach dry land. Even it meant sitting on anchor for a while!

But, understandably, Herdip wasn't too keen on the idea of sitting on anchor within reaching distance of land. David was flying out to greet us too, but he had bought a new ticket when he realised that he wouldn't be there in time. For obvious reasons, neither of us wanted to sit on the boat for a second more than necessary. And even on anchor, we would still be dangerously close to the rocks. But I just couldn't deny my parents the experience of being part of our arrival. It felt like a 'lose-lose situation'. I was close to tears and close to thumping Herdip – and it wouldn't have been surprising if she had wanted to thump me too.

I was emotionally torn. Throughout the years of planning, the weeks and months of rowing I had visualised and dreamt of every possible scenario of landing – but never once did it end like this. We would be the last boat to cross the finish line. Three other boats had gone past us in the last three days, and even though that played heavily on my competitive side, it didn't explain all of my emotions.

I had, by then, lost all the enthusiasm and determination that had previously kept me going throughout. I had no interest whatsoever in crossing the finishing line, and I just couldn't work out why I was feeling that way. In my imagination I had envisaged that reaching the finishing line would make me ecstatic, on top of the world! But at that precise moment the only emotion I felt was sadness – sadness that the adventure was all about to come to an end, and disappointment that we hadn't completed it better. I had experienced the most unique and amazing experience. But now I could only wallow in self-pity as it was all about to be over – but not in the way I had wished for. All I wanted to do now was hold my parents closely, hug them tightly – and cry. But even though they were so close, they had never felt so far away.

Unable to get my attention to check on our bearing for the finishing line, Herdip lost her temper with me. But I couldn't care less. I had lost all interest in the race, in making all the decisions, in keeping everything going. I sat there in silence, ignoring it all, as she stormed into the cabin, shouting her frustrations as she went.

With ten miles to go we contacted the Antigua and Barbados Sea Rescue (ABSR) to warn them that we were approaching. With five miles to go ABSR came out to meet us, Amanda from Woodvale with them. I sat on deck watching them approach, as Amanda waved her arms energetically in the air to greet us. I couldn't even muster the energy to greet them. Herdip came out from the cabin on hearing them approach. Slowly I started to put on my deck shoes for the last time in order to row our last few miles in *Dream Maker*. ABSR shouted directions about the tide, and told us to change direction and to aim directly for the rocks. Somewhere amongst the rocks was the entrance to Nelson's Dock. Within minutes Amanda blew the horn to mark that we had crossed the invisible finishing line ... but Mam, Dad and Gles had still not arrived from the airport. What were we to do?

The sea state was quite a bit choppier now that we were closer to the rocks, and I quickly lost control of the boat and were turned 180 degrees to be facing back to sea. Herdip joined me on the oars in the hope that more power would keep us under control. Amongst the mayhem Amanda announced over the radio that Mam, Dad and Gles had arrived! Finally! The relief! After all the worry the timing was completely perfect. We could finally row in.

Minutes later, as we approached the harbour, the air was filled with red, white and orange flares. We rowed past super-expensive yachts with their owners and crews clapping and cheering us on with their fog horns. We felt like paupers as we rowed past them.

I looked into the crowd of faces ashore. Somewhere amongst them there was Sinéad, my friend from work, Lin and Rachel from the boat *Barbara Ivy*, Herdip's boyfriend David, and of course, Dad, Mam and my sister Gles. The atmosphere was electrifying. My emotions went like a pendulum from one extreme to another, all within seconds.

Finally I got a glimpse of the Welsh flag flying, and I knew for certain that my parents were there. In my urgency to see them I forgot to slow down with the rowing and crashed loudly against the harbour wall. It felt like hours as we tried to get the oars out of their gates so that we could get close enough to jump off. I flew the Welsh flag momentarily before stepping out shakily into Dad's arms. He held me tightly and I heard a deep sigh of relief choke him. I looked straight into his eyes and realised for the first time just how much strain the crossing had caused him. Within seconds Mam and Gles had joined the tight embrace. I shivered under the emotion of the moment, unable to believe that it was all finally over.

I had fulfilled my dream! I was the first Welsh woman ever to row across the Atlantic Ocean, in 77 days, 7 hours and 37 minutes of adventure. Only forty-two women had done it before me. Herdip and I were both alive and well, and still communicating. I accepted that our friendship would probably never be the same, but I knew that we had shared a unique experience – and would always have shared respect for what we had endured together. Herdip's achievement was possibly the greater, given how hard it had been for her.

More unbelievable than our crossing, however, was the fact that our efforts had raised £190,000 towards metabolic research at the Institute of Child Health in collaboration with Great Ormond Street Children's Hospital. But amongst the hustle and bustle of the celebrations, I couldn't pride myself in our success. I was on top of the world to be reunited with my family, but deep inside I didn't feel that we deserved all the praise ... we should have done better, somehow ... cross faster, raise more money, I wasn't sure how. But in the in the pit of my stomach I knew that I hadn't given all that I had to give.

7

Adjusting to dry land

*A cloud does not know why it moves in such a direction
and at such a speed.
It feels an impulsion … this is the place to go now.
But the sky knows the reasons and the patterns behind all clouds,
and you will know, too,
when you lift yourself high enough to see beyond horizons.*
Richard Bach

I was wide awake very early the morning after our arrival in
Antigua. A hot shower followed by a dry, warm, still bed was
more pleasurable than I could have ever imagined, and
enjoying eight hours' continuous sleep was blissful. But
within seconds of being awake I longed to see the sea. In my
pyjamas therefore, I went to sit down on the beach. And
while sitting there, listening to the waves wash on the beach
by my feet, I started to cry uncontrollably. Crying like I had
never cried before. Sobbing with tears that came from the
pit of my stomach. Sobs of relief because we had succeeded.
Sobs of frustration because we hadn't done it better. Sobs
for all the worry I had caused my parents, Gles and others.
And sobs because it was all over and that I didn't have
anything on that scale to look forward to now. I really
wallowed in sobs of self-pity until finally there were no more
tears to cry. I gazed out to the horizon and I knew for certain
then that the ocean had permeated my bones.

Dad, Mam, Gles and I enjoyed an unforgettable week in
Antigua. A huge advantage of landing within minutes of

each other was that we had a full week to enjoy and explore the island, and to spend some quality time in each other's company again. Gles and I would never have gone on holiday with our parents in our thirties if it wasn't for the rowing, I'm sure. Not to a Caribbean island, for definite! The holiday was fun-filled and adventure-packed. We took our parents snorkelling, sailing and flying in a helicopter over the Montserrat volcano. Gles had her moment of fame as well when she had to kayak out to sea to rescue her little sister who had failed to master wind-surfing!

During that week, Mam and I sat on the golden sands of Antigua discussing the adventure in detail. In her worry, Mam tried to make me promise that I would never do anything like that again. She explained how difficult the experience had been, for Dad in particular.

By agreeing, and promising never to undertake such an adventure again, I would give peace of mind to the two people that loved me the most. But I couldn't. Going on oath to Mam while sitting there in the Antiguan sun would be nothing more than saying an outright lie. I knew that I would have to undertake another adventure at some point in the future. It's selfish beyond words to choose to do something that causes pain and heartache to those that love you the most. But I couldn't contemplate denying my own emotions either. Was I being selfish or preserving myself? The line between 'selfishness' and 'self-preservation' seems ever so thin.

The time came to fly home, and I couldn't believe who stood there waiting for me at arrivals in Gatwick: Jo and Lucy, with their children Mia, Henry and Rupert; Jamie, our sponsor; Dr Ashok Vellodi, Metabolic Consultant, and my PhD supervisor, Niamh, clinical nurse specialist in lysosomal storage disorders; and Michelle, physiotherapist, all stood there waiting to greet me. They had daffodils and Welsh flags with a huge banner saying 'Nautical Nurses Rule the Waves'. Jo and Lucy in particular had followed the dot across their computer screens daily, and had lived every second of the adventure with us. I could never repay them for all their love and support that had made it all possible.

Once back in Wales there was one crucial visit that had to come first: Nain had celebrated her 100th birthday two months before I departed for La Gomera. She was in good health, but given her considerable age part of me had wondered, when I said my final goodbye if I would ever see her again. But I shouldn't have worried. Nain would have never left us without seeing me back safely, I'm sure of that! It was a momentous reunion.

It is not the critic who counts, not the man who points out where the strong man stumbles or where the doer of deeds could have done them better. The credit belongs to the man who is actually in the arena, whose face is marred by dust and sweat and comes up short again and again because there is no effort without error and shortcomings, who knows the great devotion, who spends himself in a worthy cause, who at best knows in the end the high achievement of triumph and who at worst, if he fails while daring greatly, knows his place shall never be with those timid and cold souls who know neither victory or defeat.

Theodore Roosevelt

Shortly after, I was back in my luxurious office in Canary Wharf, wondering if it had all been just a dream. Sometimes I just couldn't believe that any of it had happened at all, and I often couldn't accept that it was all over. Even though my work was really interesting and challenging I found it incredibly hard adjusting to being confined to my desk for eight to nine hours a day. I had completely lost the ability to concentrate on anything for more than a couple of minutes at a time, and my mind would frequently drift back to reminisce about my days at sea and the thrill of being there. I longed to feel those extreme emotions I felt when I pushed myself physically further and further than I could have imagined possible. The enjoyments and suffering of day-to-day life just didn't compare with what I'd experienced out there on the Atlantic Ocean.

When I got an email from Tom saying that he was planning to run six marathons in six days across the Sahara I didn't think twice before deciding that I would join him. Even though I didn't enjoy running, the adventure appealed, and I desperately needed a challenge to aim for. Without a challenge to look forward to, how does one know what to aim for?

I loved to socialise with the lads that rowed in *Pura Vida* and *Ocean Summit*. They seemed to have the exact same thirst for adventure that I was now experiencing. They were dangerous company as they shared their hopes and aspirations for new and exciting adventures that they were planning, making me completely envious.

With the combination of long working hours and an over-inflated ego I wasn't training as hard as I should have been for the Sahara. After all, how hard could six days in the Sahara be after seventy-seven days on the Atlantic Ocean? Critically, I didn't train with a food regimen that would suit five to nine hours of running a day with practically no rest – a completely different routine to that on the Atlantic.

Landing in Cairo wasn't a promising start – I was soon to be informed that my bag was still sitting on the runway of Terminal 5 in Heathrow airport. Once again Gles came to the rescue and chased it up so that my bag would arrive before we were due to head out to the Sahara two days later. Checking into a family room with Tom and John but without any spare clothes or anything else was an interesting experience, to say the least!

After a nine-hour bus journey across Egypt we arrived at the race starting line. A hundred and fifty-four competitors – only thirty-six girls – from all parts of the world shared twelve-man tents surrounding a bonfire. Tom, John and I shared tent 'Aba' with nine other competitors.

Although everyone was mostly worried about the hot temperatures that we would experience in the mid-day sun, we also had to consider the plummeting temperatures that we would have to endure at night. As every competitor had to be responsible for carrying every single piece of kit needed for the week, including all the food that was necessary, most people had opted for a small and lightweight sleeping bag, and the smallest possible amount of clothing to minimise on space and weight. The race organisers weighed everyone's bag at the start line, and checked that everyone carried their survival kit for any emergency situation that might arise. I was pleased that my backpack weighed barely over 8 kilograms, especially considering that some competitors had backpacks reaching 20 kilograms. My thin sleeping bag made for a miserable night's sleep on a hard surface that was also really cold, but like everyone else I'm sure that it was the nerves of what lay ahead that stopped me from sleeping too well.

The race started at 9 am the following day, and it was great to see the Welsh flag flying proudly over the race start line: two other Welshmen were also competing. Within minutes of the starting gun going off Tom and John had raced off into the distance, leaving me at the back of the group. On that first day the ground was a little rocky, but at least it was firm ground, which made running relatively easy. The race organisers 4 Deserts had organised the event exceptionally well, and had placed a little pink flag every 20 metres or so to show the way. There was no need for navigational skills here, or a working compass even, so it was easy to spend the time day-dreaming away as I enjoyed the scenic view of the rocks on the horizon. It wasn't that different from watching waves of all shape and sizes approaching us – but these 'waves' were particularly slow-moving. Every 15 kilometres or so there were also well-organised water stations, where every runner was counted in and out according to their number. It was also an opportunity to have a quick check-over by one of the race medics if needed, or to treat the rapidly-appearing blisters.

The first day passed remarkably easily, and shortly after five hours I reached the finishing line, where the race organisers had already set up camp for our second night. I slept like a log that night, despite the hard, cold surface, and felt quietly optimistic for the next day.

The second day turned out to be much more painful. By 11 am, two hours after the race start, the temperature had reached over 40 degrees Celsius. The ground was also much softer, and now and again while climbing the dunes my short stumpy legs would sink knee-deep into soft sand. It took me over nine hours to reach camp that second night, and when I arrived I was so exhausted that I had no appetite whatsoever. I had eaten practically nothing at all that day, but my freeze-dried ration pack made me feel queasy from just looking at it.

On the morning of the third day I couldn't face breakfast either – freeze-dried porridge with strawberries, which was my favourite out on the Atlantic Ocean, now made me feel sick, and I gagged as I tried to swallow it. From the start line that day every step turned out to be one miserable step after another. I just couldn't escape to the 'happy place' in the back of my mind as I normally do when enduring such a physically challenging and painful experience. I had gaiters attached to my trainers, a piece of material that served to stop the sand from streaming in, but the glue that was holding them in place had melted away, letting what seemed like endless tons of sand gather in my trainers. As I rested every hour or so to empty out all the sand out of my socks I could no longer find rocks to rest in the shade of. By now every single step required a huge amount of effort. A two-year-old child would have probably crawled faster than I could move. After running the Snowdonia, London and Loch Ness marathons I would often joke that 'hitting the wall', to which so many runners refer, would never happen to me: I ran so slowly that I would see the wall miles beforehand and walk around it! But that third day, out in the Sahara, I was certainly too blind to see the enormous wall that was fast approaching. When the race medic drove past in the 4x4 asking if I was ok, I couldn't even formulate an answer. A little nod accepting the offer of a ride in the 4x4 was all that I could muster.

Crawling into the tent to join the other runners that night and admitting that I had failed to complete the course that day was tough. I couldn't eat anything that night either, but I was determined to try again the following morning. I forced myself to swallow a few mouthfuls of porridge and stood on the start line once more. I walked the first eight miles with an American sailor, and enjoyed his company. But shortly after reaching the first water station I started to feel nauseous, and shortly after I was vomiting. The race medics gave me some anti-emetics to help with the retching and vomiting before I stumbled on. I just couldn't rationalise why this was so unbearably difficult.

By around the fifteen-mile mark I had to take a rest every fifteen to twenty minutes, and pretty soon I was the last competitor in the race. By now I had the company of a camel and a local guide who was collecting all the pink flags. After about an hour of travelling at my snail's pace the man announced that the camel couldn't stay out in the sun for much longer! Yes, even a camel had had enough of waiting for me!

The race medic was called, and I was led without objection into the 4x4 to finish the course. Indeed, I think that I begged to be rescued. While climbing out of the 4x4 at the next water station I felt really light-headed and the nausea passed in waves. We had arrived at a famous oasis. I had been aware of the small patch of vegetation in the distance for some hours but it hadn't seemed to get any closer despite my efforts. On my arrival it seemed that I wasn't in the mood to appreciate the beauty of the oasis because I promptly passed out. As it happened there were four race medics at the water station; within minutes they had cut through my clothes, placed intravenous catheters in my arms, and were pushing fluids containing sugar and salts into my veins. They also packed ice-packs around me in a bid to bring my body temperature down. I was very confused when I finally came to, and stared blankly at the sea of faces that were around me.

I spent the rest of the afternoon resting in the medical tent, having more intravenous fluids and enjoying a can of warm Coke to restore my energy and spirit. I wasn't keen to join in on the fifth day – a sixty-mile trek which was likely to take most of the competitors over twenty-four hours to complete. I spent the day with Mohammed and the race medic in the 4x4 driving up and down the course – dispensing drugs, sweets and words of encouragement to keep all the other runners in the race. Unfortunately some, like me, had to admit that the Sahara had beaten us, and they joined us in the 4x4.

The sixth day was a five-mile sprint through the streets of Cairo before reaching the finishing line by the pyramids, and I decided to join in – but felt like a complete fraud as I was greeted by supporters and news reporters at the end.

Seeing Ryan Sandes from South Africa, the ultimate winner, and all the other runners compete had been truly inspirational. The other Welsh competitors had finished fourth and seventeenth overall, and John and Tom had also done amazingly well.

I had experienced a part of the world that few would see. Seen a different part of nature, and once again experienced true silence and the beauty of seeing the night's stars without light pollution to destroy the view. But I had also exposed myself to the drug of pushing myself to the extreme. Far from making me vow never to experience it again, I felt more passionately than ever that I *wanted* to experience it again. But maybe accepting that being a 'water-baby' was the way to go!

8

The Indian Ocean

The world is round,
and the place which may seem like the end
may also be only the beginning.
Ivy Baker Priest

I am always doing that which I can not do,
in order that I may learn how to do it.
Pablo Picasso (1881–1973)

Fourteen months after landing in Antigua, I was back sitting in an ocean rowing boat in Geraldton, Western Australia, ready to embark on another ocean crossing – the vast expanse of the Indian Ocean this time.

This was the first time ever that a race had ever been organised across the Indian Ocean, and previously only two solo rowers had ever traversed its vast expanse – one being Simon Chalk, the Director of Woodvale, who had set the race up. Just to be part of the first-ever race was, for me, phenomenal in itself.

There had been merely three months since I had received a phone call offering me the opportunity. Within days I had resigned from a good job as the worst recession in years hit, rented my flat to a tenant, and borrowed £8000 from the bank so that I could become one of the *Ocean Angels*. I had also persuaded Ollie Garrigue, a French businessman who had also been my rugby coach at London Wasps, to sponsor the rest of my race costs. As a businessman I'm sure he knew that it was a pretty lousy investment, but as a friend he was willing to sponsor me.

The *Ocean Angels* were made up of three other girls, Sarah Duff, Fiona Waller and Jo Jackson. Three girls that I didn't know, but three that shared exactly the same dream as I did – to become the first women ever to row across the Indian Ocean. Most people would regard my decision to join them at such a last minute's notice as being completely foolish, but having spent every minute since landing in Antigua yearning to be back at sea, longing to do better, I just couldn't turn down the opportunity.

But there was one crucial phone call that had to be done before I said the final 'YES' – call my parents to ask them for permission to go! To ask for their *blessing* to go, knowing how much worry and heartache the Atlantic crossing had caused, would not have been fair. But I didn't want to go completely against their wishes either. It was a painfully long twenty-four hours as I waited for their approval, without objection. With four of us in the boat, it would be less of a risk, and less of a worry – that, at least, was the hope.

This time I would be rowing in *Pura Vida*, the boat that Tom, John, Carl and Robbie had rowed into victory in the Atlantic race. Given her record I knew that she was a good boat, but her set-up was very different to *Dream Maker*. Because she was shipped out to Australia within weeks of me deciding to join the crew, however, there was no time to get familiar with her and all the equipment on board. At four feet longer than *Dream Maker* she certainly didn't offer much space to accommodate two extra rowers. I'd also arrived in Geraldton a few days later than everyone else, as I just couldn't get there any sooner, and that had also resulted in me having less time to familiarise myself with everything. But somehow none of those issues bothered me at all.

I looked out on to the shore. There was nothing comparable between Geraldton and La Gomera (from where I'd started the Atlantic race), and up until now the journey to the start line could not have been more different. So far this felt like embarking on a completely different challenge.

It was a huge advantage to join the crew so late in the day as the hard work had mostly all been done. All the planning and organising was pretty much all in place. All I had to do was turn up in Australia. The other three had also nominated a charity – Breast Cancer Care. Fiona had lost her Mum to breast cancer, and had conquered cancer herself. She had already endured so much. It was an easy choice, therefore, to be supporting this charity that was so important to her.

Despite the fact that the competing fleet was much smaller in the race there were far more people on the shoreline to see us off. From the boat they all seemed like ants jostling around on the beach. Amongst them was Shelley, my ex sister-in-law, who now lived in Australia. She had driven all the way to wish me well on our voyage, and I was really grateful to her and her family for their support.

I didn't feel any emotions as we sat there waiting for the fog horn to announce the race start. No fear, no excitement, no apprehensions, nothing. I felt completely void of emotions, just a blank canvas completely focused on doing the job at hand. It was actually a relief that I didn't have to worry about my parents on the shoreline this time round. The lambing season had started – and I was hopeful that the busiest season on the farm would keep them preoccupied and prevent them from worrying about me.

I was rowing the first two-hour shift with Jo, while Fiona and Sarah were able to enjoy some last-minute banter and goodbyes with the other crews. There were ten boats competing, four teams of four, four pairs and two solos. We were the only female competitors in the race, but we were also the only crew that had any ocean rowing experience. Fiona and Sarah had rowed in an all-female four across the Atlantic, and had arrived in Antigua three days before Herdip and me. Between the three of us we had 225 days combined experience of ocean rowing. We hoped that our experience would make up for our lack of power compared to the men, but who could know what the Indian Ocean would throw at us. Everyone had warned us that this would be a much harder experience. This race to Mauritius was nearly 700 miles longer than the Atlantic race. Determination, endless energy and a positive outlook would all be needed. That and a considerable amount of luck!

As all the ants on shore became smaller and smaller, and the chatting amongst the crews dwindled to the odd wave and thumbs-up, I looked around in amazement. I just couldn't comprehend how I, Elin, had the privilege and the opportunity to be embarking on an amazing, unique and unforgettable adventure for the second time in two years.

When you reach the end of your rope,
tie a knot in it and hang on.
Thomas Jefferson

Grasp today with all your might:
it is the tomorrow you feared yesterday.
Anonymous

The first few days on *Pura Vida* turned out to be as unbearable and horrific as those that I'd experienced on *Dream Maker*. The first two days in particular merged into one miserable, painful experience as we battled on, merely focusing on existing.

We had been warned that rowing beyond the continental shelf would be difficult, and that a land mass the size of Australia might work as a magnet, drawing us back. Things were further complicated as we had to row north around the Abrolhos islands, where the sea state, not helped by the weather, seemed to be one raging cauldron of movements. We battled against waves that approached us from every direction possible, crashing into us with such force that we were often sent flying off our seats. I was used to being thrown off my seat in the Atlantic but the might and force of these waves appeared to be even more brutal.

As the exhaustion of the first two days crept in, and we slowly came to realise that everything that had been painful and intolerable on the Atlantic would be as painful and as intolerable here on the Indian Ocean, the mood on *Pura Vida* seemed pretty quiet. Each one of us, I suspect, was praying that the bitter elements that were battering us this early on wouldn't continue to haunt us throughout the crossing.

But on the third day I slowly came to realise that one of the most dangerous elements facing us would be ourselves. The wind and the waves made everything seem agonising, and time after time we were thrown on to the deck as if we were rag dolls. But no one wanted to consider being the first to take time out – to sit on the para-anchor for a while until the weather turned in our favour.

After the Atlantic Sarah and Fiona felt that they had not been able to perform to their full potential because of crew dynamics. Like me, I think that they both loathed the idea of being part of a dysfunctional crew, and Jo, who had never rowed an ocean before, probably felt that she had to prove that she was just as capable as the rest of us. As a result I'm pretty sure that not one of us wanted to be considered the weak link in the team, and as a result nobody wanted to be the one to propose resting the bad weather out – especially this early on into the crossing. There was no alternative other than to battle on.

The news that three boats had dropped out in the first three days was a huge knock to our confidence. Could we really do this? It was even more devastating news that Roger, who was rowing with Tom in *Dream It, Do It*, had been badly injured after a rogue wave threw him off his seat.

As I approached the end of a particularly agonising shift I decided it was time to raise the issue of whether we should rest on the para-anchor for a while. In amongst the efforts to swap over safely, with the wind howling loudly round us, my proposal seemed to have been pretty much completely dismissed. Sarah and Fiona battled on with the rowing. When I stood back out on deck two hours later I knew instantly that things were no better; if anything they seemed to be worse. But I took position on the seats, too afraid to be seen as 'weak'. I decided however that I had to voice my concerns to Jo. So as the wind howled and roared around us I tried to raise my concerns. One of the huge disadvantages of rowing backwards is that it's often impossible to hear the other rower speak, and it was a problem that would trouble me frequently on this crossing.

In the condition we faced I had no alternative but to shout loudly so that Jo could hear me. I expressed my concern about our safety given the current sea state, and that I thought we should take some time out to see if things improved. I also went on to explain that I found it really difficult to talk about my concerns with Fiona, as she appeared to be against discussing the issue at all. Jo shouted back that she agreed, and felt the same way. Seconds later, before I could even think of a solution of how to move forward, Fiona appeared in the hatch door shouting, 'If you're going to talk about me, at least wait until I've gone to sleep.' The wind had betrayed us, and the issues that we were merely trying to resolve. My stomach sank with overwhelming fear that I was once again embarking on a crossing that would be full of tension. Jo and I rowed on in utter silence.

But about half an hour later a huge wave crashed into us and threw Jo viciously off her seat. In that second I knew that this was complete and utter madness, and I insisted that we stopped rowing – until we had sunrise to give us some light at least. Without further discussion, Jo and I packed away the oars and deployed the para-anchor. As we hadn't discussed it with the others to get their agreement on stopping I was worried that they would disagree and disapprove, even though I was certain that we had made the right decision from a safety point of view.

I said good-night to Jo and crawled into the bow cabin to join Sarah. For the first fifteen days we had agreed that Fiona and Jo would share the stern cabin, while Sarah and I settled into the small one in the bow. To say that the bow cabin is small is actually a huge understatement. It's much shorter than two meters in length and there isn't the slightest possibility of being able to sit upright in it. To be honest, it's more reflective of a coffin than a living quarter. To have Sarah and me, the largest two of the crew, in there together at the beginning like this was a big error of judgement – we barely fitted it, and there was hardly room to breathe! As wave after wave washed over the cabin there was just no way that we could leave the hatch door open without suffering an endless pouring of water fall in on top of us. Every now and then, when the air got too thick to breathe we would briefly open the hatch to let some air blow in, praying each time that a huge wave wouldn't catch us. Nine times out of every ten we were drenched through!

We were blown back nine miles, and being confined in that cabin with Sarah for thirty hours pushed me to the brink of madness! The heat was completely intolerable. Fiona had already experienced it during their Atlantic crossing, and Jo and I became familiar with it early into our crossing – Sarah's ability to radiate heat was a certain killer! And even though it wasn't Sarah's fault – she could do nothing about it – being confined so close to her, and the heat that she radiated, not to mention the condensation and lack of air to breathe, drove me mad. The fact that Sarah was able to lie there, in the same position, completely happy, without having to move an inch or to go to the toilet didn't help my mental state at all!

Finally the weather eased enough for us to be able to escape from our captivity. Fiona and I sat on deck to examine the damage, and cleared the air about the previous night's misunderstanding. The waves had ripped our dagger-board – a retractable keel – in half, and it was now dancing on the sea surface, being held only by the tiniest of threads. One of our oars had also been snapped in two, and our auto-helm bracket had been ripped away. Our navigation light on top of the bow cabin had also been completely ripped off. Nearly all of the deck hatches were water-filled – including the one which held our methane energy cell, which was now water-damaged beyond repair. *Pura Vida* had been through one hell of a battle, but it had managed to keep us completely safe.

It was a real sense of déjà vu when I jumped into the rough sea later that day. We had been unable to detach the dagger-board from the boat. We knew that we would not be able to fix it, given the extent of the damage, and even though we knew it would make maintaining our course on some of the bigger waves more difficult we saw no point in dragging it along with us for the ride, especially as it banged away against the hull. I decided that jumping into the sea to detach it from below was the easiest option, and that's what I did. Luckily, as soon as I swam under the boat to get hold of it and pull with all my might, it came off easily, so I was back safely on the deck in no time.

Losing the auto-helm bracket this early on was a big blow. It was a luxury rather than a necessity to have, and we had survived without one on *Dream Maker* just fine, but our steering on *Pura Vida* had been set up to incorporate it. Resetting the set-up, therefore, was problematic. Fiona didn't want the steering system to be foot-controlled as she had a weak knee, so we were left to steer our course by adjusting it by hand. In hindsight, it's clear that we would not have been able to use much of the auto-helm anyway as it requires high energy consumption, and we were now without our methane energy cell, which was incorporated as an additional system to our solar panels to increase our power availability.

But adjusting to a new steering system in those early days, while the side-effects of fatigue and exhaustion were playing a part, was difficult. It also became apparent very early on that the setting for adjusting by hand was just too far for me to reach – and my short arms and small hands haunted me once more! The steering setting was placed on the port side gunwale, which had to be adjusted by the rower in stern. To adjust our bearing, whoever was rowing in stern would have to stop rowing, tuck the oars in and lean across to reach it. I quickly realised that it was too far away for me to reach it without over-stretching towards it. Each time I'd stretch a wave would inevitably hit the boat, snatching my seat away from beneath me – leaving a big bruise on my bottom where I'd then land heavily on the sliding rails. To make matters worse it would often result in the boat being turned 180 degrees, and the losing of valuable time as we then had to re-adjust our course completely. I soon detested being responsible for the steering, with real, deep hatred.

At last we rowed past the Abrolhos Islands, and were finally able to row west rather than north-west. The weather turned in our favour, and finally things started to feel as if they were getting easier.

> *... it is not strength of body but rather strength of will*
> *which carries a man farthest,*
> *where mind and body are taxed at the same time*
> *to their utmost limit.*
> Apsley Cherry-Garrard

> *For the average man, there is the ocean –*
> *empty, beautiful, available and infinitely appealing.*
> Dr William A Nierenberg

It was a huge relief when we could finally adjust to our routine after the challenges of the first week. Sarah, Fiona and I were back in the swing of the ocean as if the Atlantic crossing had merely been a few hours before. Straight away Jo had also showed that she was just as able and strong to conform to our routine.

We had set a slightly different routine this time, compared to the two hours rowing, two hours resting routine used day after day on the Atlantic. This time we had set on a schedule of ninety minutes rowing in the mid-day sun, two hours rowing over dawn and dusk, with one four-hour rowing shift at night. We were all desperate to avoid the devastating effect of sleep deprivation that had been so brutal on the Atlantic. One rest break of four hours' completely unbroken sleep would make a world of difference, and although we acknowledged that that our rowing would not be that efficient in the four-hour shift, it was a compromise that we were all happy to accept. An ocean row is a marathon, not a sprint, after all!

Five days into the crossing we swapped rowing partners. This became a crucially important aspect, and an arrangement that made sure that we worked really well as a team. Changing rowing partners not only allowed for a change in company and in the topics of conversations shared, but it was also like a breath of fresh air, which meant that we weren't quite as easily bored with each other's company – or annoyed with each other's bad habits and bad mood swings! The dynamics between each of the pairs were quite different, from their working arrangements to their topics of conversation, and even when lying in the cabin during your rest time it was enjoyable to be eavesdropping on the latest gossip! This arrangement also stopped any division of 'us and them' that could have occurred.

Every fifteen days two rowers also swapped cabins, and moving home from the stern to the bow cabin became quite an event in our calendar. The stern cabin was large in size by comparison and offered the luxury of being able to sit up (in some form) and stretch your legs out while lying down! But the luxury came at a price! All the equipment was also fixed in the stern cabin, so the day-to-day management of the water-maker, gas cooker, battery power and plotting on the GPS was the responsibility of whoever slept in the stern.

This could often feel like a heavy burden when the desire for sleep was all-consuming! By rotating cabins in this way it meant that everyone shared the workload and responsibilities equally, whilst also sharing the misery of being confined in the bow cabin. Adjusting to clambering in and out through a two-foot hatch, in between spells of living in a box that is no larger than a coffin, takes some getting used to. But once accustomed to it you soon realise that it's the best place to be for some good-quality, undisturbed sleep!

Rather than the traditional stove usually taken for ocean rows, we had invested in jet boilers this time, as it would boil the water much quicker, and hopefully therefore use much less gas. The only problem was that they didn't come with a fixed bracket, which meant that you had to hold onto it all the time while waiting for the water to boil or the waves would throw it in every direction possible. As before, there was a fire risk from using them inside the cabin. But none of us wanted to sit out on deck using them while the other one waited patiently in the bow cabin for their food to be served! On those rare occasions that we were stupid enough to place the jet boiler down without holding on momentarily it would quickly tumble, throwing flames and hot water across the cabin. That would make sure that we wouldn't be stupid enough to put it down again – not within the same break, anyway!

The responsibility of being in the stern also involved keeping an eye on the AIS (Automatic Identification System). Rather than the Sea-Me which Herdip and I had relied on in *Dream Maker*, the AIS is a highly sophisticated piece of equipment which identifies every ship on the horizon (and beyond) and displays the name, speed and direction of travel, while warning them that we were on their radar. Vital information to support our safety, and to minimise my stress level every time I saw a ship on the horizon! But even with the AIS, I still felt twitchy and nervous whenever I knew that there was one in the vicinity – much to the amusement of the other three.

We had the same SPECTRA water-maker as that on *Dream Maker*, but it had been fitted differently. This time the outlet pipe was attached to a 20-litre tank that was placed in the galley, with an attached tap placed nearby. I found the design and set-up annoying, and just couldn't rationalise the point of spending additional time and energy pumping away at the tap to get water. It was also annoying me even more that we couldn't see how much water was in the tank. So when the water-maker was running it was impossible to see when it was full, and it would often spill over into the hatch – causing even more work. And when we were low on power supply we had no idea how to ration our water supply as we couldn't see how much we had. It is the small things, which seem so insignificant on land, that can really annoy and irritate when living in a confined space at sea.

It was the responsibility of whoever slept in the stern cabin to prepare the meals for her rowing partner. Some considerable time would always be spent discussing the menu of the day, and there would be some haggling if one rower had a more attractive option than the other on certain days. In the early days when the organisation of food packets was not as organised as it should have been I was guilty of eating the others' packs – accidentally, of course! But that was the ultimate sin, and I soon learnt not to repeat the same mistake.

Knowing how quickly one gets bored from eating the same food over and over again we had ordered a large variety of packs from three different suppliers this time. My favourite, for sure, was roasted lamb, served with mashed potatoes, peas, gravy and mint sauce. It was divine! Although I suspect that Dad would argue that the pieces of 'meat' had never been part of a live animal!

Once the meals had been prepared in their packs in the stern cabin, they would be passed down along the deck by the rowers, with the same message every time: 'More water if she wants it', 'More water if she wants it', 'More water if she wants it'. And once the pack had been stirred and inspected the message would be conveyed back: 'No it's fine as it is thanks', 'No it's fine as it is thanks', No it's fine as it is thanks'. There was nothing monotonous at all about our journey!

The most important job, and the most enjoyable by far, that was associated with being in the stern cabin was being in charge of the satellite phone and the laptop. This time I'd managed to secure the loan of an IBM laptop that I had used while competing in the Sahara race. It was light, hardcore and brilliant. Each morning after sunrise, with the porridge nearly ready for consumption, turning on the satellite phone to receive any messages and connecting to the laptop for our e-mails was the biggest pleasure of all. The seconds (often minutes) while we waited for the messages to download would drag painfully. How many messages will we receive today? We wondered. Who will they be for? What was our position in the race? How were the other competitors doing? What was the big news at home? These were the issues that preoccupied our thoughts, and influenced our topics of conversation. They were our lifeline to home.

If the weather was favourable we could open the hatch door and read out all the messages to the pair rowing, who would then convey it all to whoever was in the bow cabin. Welsh messages for me would complicate this arrangement slightly, of course. Swine flu, the recession and the death of Michael Jackson were the key events that seemed to occupy world-wide news. Receiving messages from home once again became a crucial fix to lift our spirits, and there would be some considerable discussion on the news received. When things appeared to be unbearably tough, a message from home could transform everything, recharge our batteries and give that much-needed boost to keep us going.

Another daily ritual that amused us greatly was writing our blog. Our intention from the start was to provide a humorous, light-hearted account of our adventures for our friends, family and supporters. We didn't want to bore them with the reality of twelve hours of rowing, and we certainly didn't want to worry them with the reality of the situations that we occasionally faced. Laughing at our self-imposed circumstances would certainly help to put the right perspective on things. And although it was difficult at times to find the enthusiasm or imagination for a daily light-hearted account, the response we got from people back home made it easier to persevere with the writing. The fun that we had writing the blog made carrying the laptop along well worthwhile.

The other event that gave much fun and amusement were our fashion parades! Especially before we'd go out for dinner! Eating in the bow cabin was never that easy, especially in rough seas. You'd have to attempt eating while lying on your front and the meal would often sit undigested in your stomach for some time after. Occasionally, to break from the hum-drum daily routine, whoever was in the bow cabin would go and visit the person in the stern cabin for dinner. This journey of a few meters would be a big event in the diary, and being like all other girls, we would often get dressed up for the occasion! As we rowed naked most of the time (as the salt would become a thin crust on our clothes) even wearing underwear was quite an event. Sarah in particular had packed some really pretty underwear, and she was brilliant at modelling them all as she hobbled over the oars and wobbled across the deck! There was much *ooing* and *ahing* as we admired the selection of the day (even though we all only had two or three to choose from) and a lengthy and interesting conversation inevitably followed.

> *An agreeable companion is as good as a carriage.*
> Publius Syrus (42 BC) Maxim, 143

> *Second helpings are what happiness is all about.*
> Winnie the Pooh

Rowing with Sarah was an extremely joyful experience. I had never met anyone just like Sarah before, and I suspect that I will never meet anyone else as happy and optimistic about life as she is. In whichever situation we found ourselves, Sarah would always manage to bring a smile to my face, with her quirky sayings and tuneful singing! 'Brr! It's a bit Arctic!' would be one of her daily sayings as she'd step out, naked, on to the deck. That and, 'Stop it! I don't like it!' to the sea, in the most girly voice that you could imagine, as another wave washed over us. It seemed that Sarah lived permanently on a pink, fluffy, happy cloud, regardless of whether our actual situation was serious, sensible, dull or in danger. Frequently, while rowing with Sarah, it would be very little effective rowing that I would actually be able to do, as I'd be laughing too much to row. Sarah also started to learn Welsh, and one of our favourite games to pass away the time would be to count every other number to 100 in Welsh, English and French, 'un, two, troi, pedwar, five, six.'

One of the most vivid memories that I have of the Indian row that is likely to stay with me forever is that of rowing with Sarah for four solid hours, in the most intolerable squall in the darkest night that I have ever experienced. The rain didn't ease at all, and the wind howled continuously. But by this point, there was an understanding amongst the four of us. Four hours' continuous, unbroken sleep, on your own in the cabin was blissful – sacred! And in the worst weather, therefore, if we weren't actually in danger, the unspoken rule was that we'd stay out to row. The rule was unspoken but carved in slate! But without Sarah's joyful company I would have never been able to continue with that shift that night. The two of us imagined what our Mum's opinion would be if they could just see us! Mam would be distraught and disgusted in equal measures, I'm sure; nothing more than pointless suffering!

We couldn't keep our eyes open as the rain fell in streams over our faces, and keeping a conversation going was near impossible as the wind stole every sentence. We both started to sing in a bid to compete with the elements around us. I was completely out of tune and couldn't remember the words to any song, but continuing with the singing was just as important as continuing with the rowing that night. That and enjoying a full chocolate bar, on the hour, every hour! Eating was by far the biggest pleasure on board by now, and apart from the actual joy of eating, the discussions around what to eat, when to eat, and the food that we missed the most occupied otherwise long, dull hours. With four chocolate bars each to enjoy daily we could never be sad for long!

But the usual laughter, the raucous singing, and the trilingual counting that Sarah and I enjoyed wasn't appreciated by all. And while Sarah and I could also both fall asleep easily, poor Fiona and Jo couldn't. So all the noise and racket that we created on deck would frequently keep them awake, unfortunately! Sarah and I were certainly the naughty kids on tour!

Within two weeks of being out at sea we were at the front of the fleet – and nobody could quite believe that a bunch of girls were leading! By now four boats had been rescued, leaving just six of us left, all separated over a huge distance.

The four of us had adjusted well to the routine, and were enjoying the favourable weather that we were now blessed with. It was a huge advantage, and made life so much easier as we cruised in the right direction. For the next couple of weeks we were flying! We just couldn't believe how well we were doing, and at times it actually felt that it all seemed too easy! All four of us had longed to do well, and had feared that we would be left at the back of the fleet by miles. But never in our wildest dreams had we imagined that we would be at the front! But that's how it was for three weeks and more. None of the physical suffering even registered, or bothered us in the least as we prided ourselves in our position! To amuse ourselves we even designed the dress that each of us would wear for receiving the BBC Sports Personality Team of the Year category! Oh what fun we had as our imagination ran riot!

The greatest joy of nature is the absence of man.
Bliss Carman

Exploration is the physical expression of the intellectual passion.
Apsley Cherry-Garrard

I would spend hours day-dreaming while gazing at the clouds above. The shapes that the wind would form in the clouds would also be a fascinating topic of conversation, as our imagination once again ran wild. The other three were far superior to me – it seemed never-ending in terms of what they claimed that they could see! At dusk, as the sun disappeared over the horizon, I loved watching the clouds take on shades of pink and orange, which would be reflected in the sea. The colours were incredibly beautiful and a welcome change to our normal world of blue.

At night we also gazed at the stars. Fiona had brought star charts with her, and it was particularly satisfying to spot the Southern Cross and Orion himself above us. Occasionally, on a particular clear night, without a cloud in the sky at all, I was sure that I could see some of the planets.

We had arranged to receive the weather forecast and sea state over email as well. Following the arrival of our forecast there would be much discussion on which route to take. And it was based on this information that we would start our hunt for eddies. Eddies are huge surface of water that flow in circular patterns, which flow in directions differing from, and at some points contrary to, the direction of the larger-scale current seen in the sea. As the water often moves at some speed our hope was to 'hitch a ride', making sure that we jumped off the ride before it started to head back towards Australia.

Our hunt would often take us away from the direct line of travel, which would be clearly shown on everyone's computer screen back home. This would obviously cause some considerable confusion to our supporters. Given the messages that we were receiving they clearly thought 'Typical women! Can't read a map!' And God knows – there was no one out there to ask for directions!

For a while our hunt was a huge success and it seemed that we cruised from the edge of one eddy to the next. But the Indian Ocean clearly didn't want us to have it so easily all the way across and soon enough our luck ran out. The elements turned against us, and we were soon fighting to find an escape route. Once again we were confined for days.

Around the seventh week I also started to suffer from the hardship of confinement and rowing. I'd wake up from each break with an excruciating headache, and while climbing out through the hatch door I'd often feel light-headed. Occasionally I'd fall over, in a nose-dive fashion, only barely avoiding a nasty fall. My clumsy state was far from ideal given the constant threat of falling overboard, but I just couldn't figure out what the problem was. It was too late into the trip for it to be some sort of motion-sickness-related thing, and it couldn't really be attributed to sleep deprivation as I had adjusted much better to the routine this time. Eventually we realised that the gas canisters, attached to the jet boilers, were leaking. Due to the damp environment it seemed the connection point had corroded and gas was leaking into the cabin. Given the size of the cabin, and the lack of air that flowed through it, the smallest amount of gas would have caused a headache. It was a huge relief when it was finally my turn to move from the stern cabin and all its responsibility to the bow cabin. I could rest more there, without any gas polluting the air, and without any responsibilities – apart from dispensing the toilet paper! All of our toilet paper supply was stored in the bow cabin, and it was the very important job of the person in that cabin to dispense it to all that came to visit the big purple bucket. The negotiation process that ensued resulted in tears of rage and laughter!

Rowing can be an extremely enchanting process. Slide

forward, arms stretched out, straight whenever possible in the sea state. Gently dropping the oars in the water before starting on the movement of pushing back with your legs, all the power being slowly transferred from the soles of the feet through the knees and into the thighs, carefully drawing the oars close to your abdomen. No jerky movements, just one graceful manoeuvre. That's the aim, anyway! And given the simplicity of it, and the hours spent practising one would imagine that I had would have perfected the art. But in reality my mind would wander and the boat would jolt in random directions depending on the waves, so each stroke was actually completely different. But throughout it all the body would somehow automatically react and adapt so that the rowing could continue, all be it without much finesse. But around the seventh week I completely lost the ability to row effectively.

The elements had been against us for some time and the rough sea state made hard work of the rowing. Once again our hands were sore and suffering, especially as I tried to keep control of the oars in rough water. They'd become claw-shaped early on in the trip this time and once again the oars would crash onto our shins, leaving them bruised. Fiona in particular was suffering and had an open wound which just wouldn't heal. But the problem that was haunting me the most this time was an excruciating pain in my right elbow. Every time as I pushed into back stop on my seat, and feel the resistance increasing in my arms, a sharp pain would shoot up my arm. To try to minimise it I started to row with my elbow bent, in an angle. I knew that I wasn't rowing effectively that way, but I couldn't cope with the pain. Once again I didn't want to appear to be weak.

But knowing that I wasn't rowing well, or effectively, I started to worry that the others would notice, and be critical of my efforts and contribution. With every sentence whispered I was sure that they were expressing their disappointment in me and so I was desperate to escape to the bow cabin for more than one reason. I could hide there from the big bad world! And was less likely to be scorned for my poor rowing technique. In reality there is nowhere to hide on an ocean rowing boat – but the bow cabin gives you that tiny amount of privacy which makes you feel that there is!

The only relief we had by now was the fact that the RowTec seats that were fitted were much more comfortable than those that we had on *Dream Maker*. And even though my skin had salt sores I wasn't experiencing any of the pressure pains that had been so debilitating on the Atlantic. Having adjusted well to the routine early on, and got over the initial exhaustion and sleep deprivation we didn't always need to sleep on every break. To pass away the time and to avoid the risk of thinking too much, I read. Early on I'd finished reading my book of choice for the journey, *The Longest Climb*, which recounted the tales of Dominic Faulkner and his team mates as they cycled from the Dead Sea to the bottom of Everest before going on to scale Everest itself. It was a really interesting book and just like reading Ranulph Fiennes' autobiography *Mad, Bad and Dangerous* while I was on the Atlantic, it motivated and inspired me to keep going. I also read the book that Sarah had chosen for the journey, *Pillars of the Earth*. It was a long and exciting novel which got me enthralled. The only problem was that even when I needed sleep I just couldn't put the book down. I'd immediately regret it when it was time to get back on the oars, and my poor rowing companion would probably be cursing as much as they tried to keep me awake at the oars!

But the weather deteriorated further, and all of a sudden there didn't seem to be time to read or to worry about the others' opinion of me and my rowing. Now it seemed that all we could think about was surviving.

Nothing in the world can take the place of persistence.
Talent will not: nothing is more common than unsuccessful
men with talent.
Genius will not: unrewarded genius is almost a proverb.
Education will not: the world is full of educated derelicts.
Persistence and determination alone are omnipotent.
Anonymous

Everyone had warned us that the scorching sun of the Indian Ocean would be unbearable. And on odd days here and there, that was true. But those days seemed very few and far between, as we moved from one low weather system to another. Personally I wasn't too bothered about the sun, even though a bit of a sun tan would have been a good souvenir from the trip. My memories of the scorching Sahara sun and its impact on me was still very vivid in my mind, and the hot days that we'd experienced in the Indian Ocean had been tough for me. But fighting against miserable weather day after day and worrying continuously about our lack of power supply wasn't proving to be much fun either.

The elements were proving themselves to be much harder on the Indian Ocean than we had experienced on the Atlantic, no doubt about it. I constantly had a thick layer of salt on my skin and could taste it on my lips continuously. I'm not sure if it has any scientific merit but I wondered whether the Indian Ocean was so much saltier because the Gulf Stream didn't flow through it to dilute it.

But it wasn't just us suffering: our equipment also started to fall apart. Even though the ball bearings on our sliding seat were made from titanium they soon eroded away, and even though we'd packed spares we were soon without replacements. It took a bit of intuitive thinking to come up with an alternative solution that kept our rowing seats sliding. We were certainly lucky to have Jo and her engineering-hat on board, even if a deck looked more like a bomb-site of tools as we worked through it.

The biggest cruelty of the Indian Ocean, however, was that there was no obvious pattern as to which conditions were best to row in. Well, not one that was apparent to me, anyway. Every ocean rower's dream is to have consistent wind with large rolling waves travelling towards your destination. That way, the wind and the waves carry you speedily along, in a comfortable manner. And it was a brilliant sensation when you surfed down a big wave at high speed, each rower trying to record a top speed! A completely calm, flat sea can also be favourable for rowing. But out there on the Indian Ocean there just didn't appear to be any particular condition that would allow us to row well. Occasionally, in the calmest of seas where it was possible to see your reflection in the water, we just couldn't row at all. Instead we'd go round and round in circles, unable to make an inch towards Mauritius.

It was that sort of day on 6 June. We had around 1,200 miles left before reaching our destination, and we were starting to feel deflated with the lack of consistent progress that we were now experiencing. We'd been experiencing bad weather for some time, and had been longing for much-needed sun to boost our power supply. In the boat battery and in our bones! We hadn't seen a dolphin, whale or shark for weeks. Indeed there appeared to be no wildlife at all.

Apart from the odd albatross that would keep us company now and again it seemed that we were very much alone. Even seeing a rainbow in the sky had lost its appeal, as rainbow after rainbow had failed to meet its promise of better weather. We really needed something to boost morale.

It was on one of the sunniest days that we'd experienced in a very long time that we found ourselves once again spinning round in circles. So while the sun cheered us up, our lack of rowing progress haunted us. We gazed at the sea, with its still crystal-blue like appearance and our reflection so clearly seen. Jo and I had already been into the water to clean the hull, and to have the opportunity to enjoy something other than rowing. It was Jo, aka action-Jackson, who then led the way in climbing onto the cabin roof before diving in. I followed suit, and pretty soon we had abandoned all sense of safety and responsible behaviour and all jumped into the sea together – abandoning *Pura Vida* to drift alone without its crew. It was complete stupidity considering that a tiny bit of breeze could have blown her away from our reach, but such was the temptation to enjoy the moment that none of us dared consider it. The beauty of gazing into the depth of the sea with its beautiful array of blues was indescribable. And the realisation that we had 3,500 metres of sea below us, over a thousand miles between us and land, and God knows how many miles above us, was magical. The experience was serene, and a real boost which energised us all.

Having not seen a ship for over six weeks (we were some considerable distance away from the shipping lanes) we were really surprised to spot a tanker on the horizon. We laughed for some time, wondering what the crew would say if they knew that there were four naked 'Angels' swimming within about three miles of them.

Due to the miserable weather we had now dropped to second position in the fleet. It had been particularly depressing to watch our lead of hundreds of miles dwindle as the *Bexhill Boys*, who had taken a more northerly position, took the lead while enjoying more favourable weather, leaving us fighting our way out of yet another low weather system. Shortly after dropping to the second position we were fighting against one of the other crews, named *Row4Prostate*, not to be third. Dropping to third position would have been too much of a disappointment after the delight of leading for so long. All of a sudden it all just seemed so unfair.

During one of my weekly phone calls home, while discussing our progress and race position with my Dad, I just couldn't believe it when he said 'But they're men, Elin, you didn't really expect to beat them?' Poor Dad! I sensed that he regretted his comment before he'd even finished his sentence. Our expectations on *Pura Vida* were very high by now. And whereas completing the race would have been sufficient during those first frightening days, we now had expectations for the best place on the podium!

Around the same time news came through that *Old Mutual Endurance* had retired from the race. After fifty-three days battling against the elements I couldn't imagine a more gut-wrenching experience than dropping out of the race. But Simon Prior was braver (depending on your definition of the term!) than us and had ventured across alone. By now half of the fleet had retired from the race. That in itself spoke volumes about the conditions that we were facing.

On a journey of a hundred miles, ninety is but half way.
Dihareb Tsineaidd

Our last 400 miles were like a nightmare that I just couldn't wake up from. At the same time there appeared to be a cyclone travelling up the east African coast and we were caught on its peripheries. Powerful gale force winds blew from the south. Facing windward would make breathing difficult, such was its force. It was bitterly cold, and the wind caused waves the size of three- or four-storey houses to crash down, dumping tons of water over us and pushing us towards the sea bed. After each breaking wave a battle would ensue between *Pura Vida* and the water on the deck. For minutes, which seemed like a lifetime, we would sit in water above our waistline, helplessly watching our equipment being washed away to sea. Each second I'd pray that the boat design was stronger than the force of the breaking wave and that we'd surface above the water line soon. The sea state was unlike anything I had ever experienced before. Other waves, slightly less in height but travelling at greater speed, would hit us with such force that *Pura Vida* would be tilted onto an awkward angle, mercilessly throwing both rowers off their seats. It would only be the spare oars that were positioned as railings on either side that would prevent us from being washed away. As the conditions became more and more perilous our falls became more and more frequent, and time after time we were shaken by the sheer force of the ocean.

While helplessly watching the fierce waves approaching time would stand still as fear took hold. There was nothing that could be done, apart from holding as tightly as we could to the side and tilting our heads at the last second to avoid a face-full of raging sea. During the rough weather, while trying to swap position with Jo for my break a huge wave rose and started to approach at speed. The array of blues that shone through was breathtaking and I gazed in amazement at the beauty of the wave above us. The beauty of the colours hid the dangers that ensued. Jo in particular was in danger as she stood there barefooted and without an ankle-leash to attach her to the boat. At the last second, as all the water crashed over us she threw herself towards me, and held on to me for dear life.

By now I was seriously losing the will to get back on the oars time after time, wave after wave. I had already proved to myself that I could persevere, but what did persevering in those elements prove? Bravery or stupidity?

By now Fiona and I felt the same about the risks that we were facing, and we'd take the decision to batten down the hatches now and again. In the darkness of the night in particular we knew that we were taking unnecessary risks. If one of us was to be washed away at night there would be absolutely no chance at all of attempting a rescue attempt.

Having to rest on para-anchor so close to the finish line was infuriating. But when a rogue wave crashed Sarah against the gunwale we knew within seconds that we had no other option. Sarah screamed in pain as her ribs took the force of the collision. Given the bruises that appeared later it looked like that she may have cracked one or two, and even if she had found the courage to take to the oars again after such an experience the pain would not have allowed her to. We had no alternative than to let Sarah rest in the stern cabin, with plenty of pain-killers. When the weather allowed Jo, Fiona and I embarked on a new schedule of one hour resting for two hours rowing.

After ten weeks of an already gruelling routine the new demands were a killer. The southerly winds that followed each wave that washed over us were bitterly cold, leaving us frozen to the bones. A one-hour break just wasn't enough time to dry, let alone rest and warm up. The salt was now permanently encrusted all over my skin, as I just didn't have the energy to wash it off during break times. The temptation to snuggle up to Sarah and her ever-radiating heat was now a hugely tempting option. But as she could hardly move because of the pain it wasn't fair to squash into the cabin with her.

As we were now wet and cold twenty-four hours a day the skin on my bottom began to break down again, and as the salt penetrated into the wounds the burning painfully returned.

With less than two hundred miles to go, we were once again trapped. Despite being on para-anchor we were blown back fourteen miles in horrendous weather. Things continued to deteriorate, and the four of us were confined in the cabins. But as the weather went from bad to worse, Jo and I, now sharing the bow cabin, became seriously worried about our safety. The para-anchor was attached to a cleat on the roof of our cabin. As the wind increased the noise of the rope pulling on the cleat became increasingly loud. The whole weight of the boat being pulled by fierce winds against a para-anchor that was full with raging water was a worrying battle and we feared that the roof of our cabin would be ripped off as a consequence. We were also concerned that we were at risk of capsizing with the para-anchor becoming a pivot. As we lay in the cabin listening to the storm rage outside, and unable to sleep, my mind swirled with all the potential catastrophes that could happen given our vulnerable position. Idle time is disastrous for allowing negative thoughts and fear to run riot.

Although we didn't want to be blown back an inch more we decided that we were no longer safe on the para-anchor. In the darkness of the night, we ventured outside to haul it in. Jo's shoes had been washed away to sea some days previously and so she slid around on the deck barefooted. The para-anchor was heavier than ever, and the rope ripped through our hands as the waves battled to keep it in the sea. The wind screeched loudly in our ears, and each wave appeared to be set on casting us to the depth of the sea.

I wore a head-torch and in a minute of madness I glanced upwards. A bright silver line glistened as a wave broke above us. I instantly looked away in horror and tried to focus on breathing calmly and pulling in the rope, inch by inch, ignoring the tons of water crashing down around us.

Between both our efforts we finally had the para-anchor out of the sea and back on deck before we quickly disappeared back into the relative safety of the cabin, my heart thumping uncontrollably.

Even though Jo was a great cabin companion, small and thoughtful, there was no way to sleep through the horror. The condensation, the lack of fresh air and the noise from outside made it impossible. Where the navigation light had been attached to the cabin roof there was now a hole which allowed the sea to drip in. Everything was sodden, including our sleeping bags. When the air became too heavy to breathe we would be forced to open the hatch, exposing us to a hurling of water that would soak us further. Thank God that Jo was good company those days. The silence was comfortable when there was nothing to say, and the conversation was interesting when we felt like chatting. The experience bonded our friendship, and Jo probably knows me better than anyone now.

I think that Jo emerged as the strongest member of our team during our crossing. She would always be early for her shift on the oars, and those precious moments would be more valuable than gold, and she'd often share her chocolate too! The only sign that Jo felt a bit low would be if she wore mascara! I had been outraged that we even had mascara on the boat, but for Jo a little bit of glam from her mascara gave her a much needed boost! The mascara meant that she didn't cry once, which was quite an achievement given our situation. Our team mantra of 'Three cries and you're out' certainly worked on this crossing.

A few days earlier my Dad, Mam and Gles had flown out to Mauritius to eagerly await our arrival. Once again predicting when we would land had been impossible, and this time I was convinced that they would be flying home while we would be blown hundreds of miles north of Mauritius.

Our efforts to row west were futile. For every twenty miles that we travelled in a westerly direction we were pushed eight miles north. Reaching the finishing line in Mauritius was even more challenging than Antigua given the number of coral reefs and other surrounding islands. Being blown north was the worst thing that could happen to us. Our rowing power of two knots south had no chance in hell against forty-knot winds that were blowing us north.

Our spirits on *Pura Vida* were rock bottom, and unlike anything we'd previously experienced as we realised that we'd fail to hit the Woodvale race finishing line. Sarah was still in excruciating pain and unable to move in the cabin, while Jo, Fiona and I were barely holding it together on an hour's rest for every two hours of rowing. It was unbearable to see Sarah, who had been so happy throughout, now in such a low given the pain. To add to our suffering we no longer had any gas left, which meant that we had no hot drink or food to keep us going in our cursed position.

For a while we considered sitting it out on para-anchor for a week to allow for the bad weather to pass. In more favourable conditions we could correct our bearing. What would one extra week at sea be, after doing eleven? But in reality we knew that we just couldn't. Jo's parents, Sarah's Mum and Fiona's friend Becks were all with my parents and Gles waiting for us, and we just couldn't expect them to wait indefinitely. Once again I was being forced to adapt my expectations. A place on the podium didn't seem important any more compared with putting an end to the nightmare that we were living.

We had no option other than to head for a longitude line of 57° 37' 30, which would give us a world first record – but no position in the race. No other all-female crew had ever rowed across the Indian Ocean before and by crossing that longitude we would claim that record, and also set a record for the fastest all-female crossing! I knew that all four of us had given everything that we possibly could have, and had succeeded in overcoming brutal conditions. I couldn't have dreamt of being part of such a determined and lively crew if I'd worked with them preparing for it for years. The adventure was a huge success in that respect, and we'd also raised over £23,000 for Breast Cancer Care. The total amount raised was nothing compared to the Atlantic, and we didn't even have a position in the race, but I felt completely satisfied with what we had achieved. It had been a real honour to be one of the Ocean Angels.

Pura Vida had lived up to its name. The Costa Ricans use the expression *Pura Vida* to denote the ideology of a strong community spirit, determination and perseverance in the face of adversity – while maintaining a joyful spirit, celebrating every stroke of luck, be it big or small.

As the numbers on the GPS announced our world record, we didn't celebrate. The crossing had been 78 days, 15 hours and 54 minutes of amazing experiences. But there was no option now other than call the race organisers and ask them to help us to travel 6 miles south to Mauritius. After 3,339 miles we had been beaten by as little as 6 miles! *Six miles!* The situation was painfully hilarious. But there was no point in arguing the point with the elements. No amount of tears or pleading would have made a blind bit of difference in that gale force wind.

It wasn't the finish that any of us had foreseen or wished for, and waiting for the rescue boat was a sullen affair. But eventually as I stood on the deck, being pulled at speed by the rescue boat, I enjoyed for the last time the feeling of having huge waves wash over me, knowing that the luxuries of a hot shower, dry clothes, a warm bed and a hot cup of coffee were imminent. Not to mention the warm embrace of my family.

If the long wait for the rescue boat was difficult for us, it must have been unbearable for all our friends and family, who had no idea what state we were in. They patiently waited at the sailing club in Mauritius until three in the morning and cheered into the darkness once they knew we were close by. Fireworks and flares lit the night sky as we neared.

'Auntie Elin!' was one of the first greetings that I heard from the darkness of the crowd and I just couldn't believe it when Ilan Aled and Sara Fflur, my niece and nephew, appeared on the pontoon to greet me. It was an amazing surprise, and the hugging that followed was never-ending. I was incredibly pleased that Gles had brought them out to Mauritius to be part of the experience – which I hope they'll treasure forever, as I will.

9

Heading for home – the best journey of all

*The trouble with the rat race is
that even if you win, you are still a rat.*
Lily Tomlin

*We shall not cease from exploration,
And the end of all our exploring
Will be to arrive where we started,
And to know the place for the first time.*
T. S. Eliot

Barely forty-eight hours after reaching land I was flying back home to Wales. Gles had booked a ticket for me to travel home with them, and after a lot of worry that I would miss the flight that I was booked on, it was a relief to be able to join them – even if it did mean that I wasn't able to relax and enjoy Mauritius.

It felt odd not having Nain waiting for me at home this time round, but being back in her home, in which my parents now lived, was comfortably familiar, and a reassurance that not much had changed while I was away.

Soon after my arrival the National Eisteddfod descended on Bala. The Eisteddfod is a traditional festival which dates back to the twelfth century, celebrating the rich culture of literature, music and performance in Wales. Eighty thousand people came to enjoy the festival, and the contrast to the peace of *Pura Vida* and its population of four was a huge shock to my system.

My parents' house was a hive of activity as twenty-one friends and family stayed with us, or in caravans in the garden. I was grateful that my old friend Esther Eckley was with me, and enjoyed escaping the noise for a run or a bike ride by the lake or in nearby fields. The beauty of Llyn Tegid and the Arennig Fawr mountain delighted me as if it was the first time I'd cast my eyes upon them.

Amongst the huge crowds I was particularly fortunate to bump into Aled Gwyn, one of Wales' leading strict-metre poets, and was hugely impressed with his poetic talents when he spontaneously honoured me with an *englyn*:

> *Un lawen yw Elin Haf – yn ei mêr*
> *Mae y moroedd garwaf,*
> *Un olau, y goreuaf*
> *Rhwyfwraig yr aig, lodes braf.*

> (Elin Haf is joyful – in her marrow
> Rests the roughest ocean,
> She's fair, among the best.
> Oarswoman of the brine, a fine girl.)

Aled Gwyn captured the essence of what the ocean now meant to me, while others just wanted to know if I'd 'got it out of my system'. In truth, it feels as if the ocean is part of who I am now. My only regret is that I didn't start such adventuring much earlier in life.

Far too soon the high of being back on land, and enjoying daily comforts, faded, and the thrill of what we'd achieved on the Indian Ocean was also fading at a dramatic rate. Settling back into the daily routine can be comforting, but it can also be particularly depressing. I was poor financially but felt incredibly fulfilled by the experiences I'd shared with the other Angels. Sadly, however, nothing on land reflected that, or even compared. From the highest of highs to the lowest of lows. Apart from the loan in the bank and the scars on my bottom there was no sign of what we had experienced.

For a while, I had to rely on Gles for clothes and money. As always she was outstanding in her sisterly support, but I hated having to be reliant on anyone. As much as I hated it a cloud of self-pity loomed over me, and I longed for a challenge that would give me the feeling of elation that comes from having adrenaline run through my veins, from feeling that you're achieving something.

Memories of our time at sea occupied my thoughts continuously, and although I knew that I should move on, I was finding it practically impossible to engage with normal day-to-day things. By now nobody around me really wanted to listen to the same old rowing story, over and over again. Solo circumnavigator Pete Goss describes it perfectly in his book *Close to the Wind* – 'Back in England I stepped ashore with the impression that people were listening to me but not really hearing – the usual feeling after a long time at sea … I felt displaced for quite some time'.

Many adventurers report similar emotions, holiday blues on a greater scale. An interview with an astronaut which I read recently echoed the same. When asked how he coped with the splashdown after his experience, he answered, 'Nothing can ever compare with or live up to the experience from my journey'.

And even though I hadn't been anywhere near his personal 'paradise' I could relate to the sentiment.

According to the 2008 Ofcom report the average British citizen watched three hours and 45 minutes of television daily. And although Nain has increased the odds slightly, if I live until I'm eighty-one years old it's likely that I will have spent eleven years watching television. And according to the neuro-scientist David Eagleman it's likely that I will also spend six days cutting my nails, fifteen months searching for various lost items, eighteen months queuing, thirty-four days longing, and four weeks sitting at home wondering if there's something better that I should be doing with my time. Looking at statistics like this makes it easy for me to justify my choice of spending twenty-two weeks of my life rowing oceans. A good investment of time even.

Commuting to university in the London rat-race and sitting in front of a desk from nine to five seemed to be sucking every ounce of energy out of my life. I had two very fixed and clear projects to be working on: completing my PhD and getting my job back at the European Medicine Agency (EMA). These were the goals I was now aiming for. I knew that the work back at EMA would be challenging and satisfying, so I signed up for a French course in Brittany to prepare for the French entry exam, which I would need to pass this time. I desperately tried to focus on a challenge of intellect rather than strength. But for a long time my body felt restless and my brain felt dysfunctional as I sat staring blankly at meaningless words on my computer screen.

In many ways there are a lot of similarities between rowing an ocean and completing a PhD. An investment of time and money. Enjoyment, exasperation, and an ever-present longing to reach the finish line. Ocean rows and thesis writing just require perseverance, wave after wave, word after word, until ultimately determination becomes the foundation of success. When the time finally came to have the viva defence of my thesis, and to rejoin my old colleagues in the paediatric team at the EMA, I felt the thrill of having achieved another challenge – even though it was a very different experience from that of having pushed myself to the boundaries of my physical limits.

Don't measure yourself by what you have accomplished,
but by what you should have accomplished with your ability.
John Wooden

The definition of 'success' is a PhD thesis topic in its own right. Many base it on the amount of money they have in the bank, the speed of their car, the smile of a loved one, or the happiness of their children. But the way that I measure my own level of success is from trying to rise to new and different challenges. That's what makes me feel alive. Choosing a challenge that I would be sure to succeed in wouldn't give the same satisfaction, of course. As expressed by Nelson Mandela: 'There is no passion to be found playing small – in settling for a life that is less than the one you are capable of living'. Everybody's dream and their way to achieving those dreams are vastly different. That's what makes the world so interesting. But by setting myself a new challenge, or a different goal, is how I savour the life I've been given.

In October 2009, having rowed the Welsh Dragon across 5,691 of sea miles, equating to nearly a quarter of the way around the world, I was given the biggest acknowledgment I could have ever imagined, with an award for Services to Wales presented by the Welsh Assembly. My efforts over the years had raised nearly £250,000 for charities, and in the elegance of Glyn Llifon Hall I was honoured to meet the then First Minister of Wales, Rhodri Morgan, where I was presented with an engraved Welsh crystal vase.

Mam, Dad and Gles joined me for the day to celebrate with lunch and champagne. I knew that they were proud of what I had achieved – although Mam would be equally proud if I could just settle down and start a family! But I was delighted that they were with me for the celebration. The award was as much theirs as mine, for all their love and heart-wrenching concern that is an inevitable part of my adventures. It is sharing all of life's experiences with true friends and family that makes everything the more magical, and I'll be forever indebted to all those important people in my life.

I'm well aware that I've had an incredibly easy life, and the only challenges that I've ever had to face are those that I've set myself. Each time, I've been able to choose the type of challenge, and the level of difficulty. Not everyone is as fortunate, and some are left to overcome challenges that are forced upon them. Just like Mia and Henry and all the other children that I met during my clinical nursing days. They are the real examples of resilience, determination and perseverance in overcoming the odds, and I will forever be able to draw a lot of strength from having witnessed first-hand the way that they overcome real life challenges. It is the inspiration that I need to continue working with passion in my chosen career while also thinking what – never 'if' – my next personal challenge will be.

With the pull of the ocean continuously calling, completing a hat-trick of oceans has become my next goal – but using sails rather than oars this time. I may have spent twenty-two weeks at sea, but many people forget that I have no idea of how to sail. Learning the technical aspects of sailing has therefore become my next venture. Under the command of RORC Commodore Andrew McIrivine and his experienced crew I'll be competing in the 2011 Rolex Fastnet race, before taking on the might of the Pacific Ocean as part of the Clipper 11-12 Round the World Yacht Race. No doubt this, too, will be rewardingly challenging!

You are never too old to set another goal
or to dream a new dream.
C. S Lewis

Not all who wander are lost.
J. R. R. Tolkein

Ar Fôr Tymhestlog
Evan Evans (1795–1855)

Ar fôr tymhestlog teithio 'rwyf
I fyd sydd well i fyw,
Gan wenu ar ei stormydd oll –
Fy Nhad sydd wrth y llyw.

Drwy leoedd geirwon, enbyd iawn,
A rhwystrau o bob rhyw,
Y'm dygwyd eisoes ar fy nhaith –
Fy Nhad sydd wrth y llyw.

Er cael fy nhaflu o don i don,
Nes ofni bron cael byw,
Dihangol ydwyf hyd yn hyn –
Fy Nhad sydd wrth y llyw.

Ac os oes stormydd mwy yn ôl,
Ynhadw gan fy Nuw,
Wynebaf arnynt oll yn hy –
Fy Nhad sydd wrth y llyw.

A phan fo'u hymchwydd yn cryfhau,
Fy angor, sicr yw;
Dof yn ddiogel trwyddynt oll –
Fy Nhad sydd wrth y llyw.

I mewn i'r porthladd tawel clyd,
O sŵn y storm a'i chlyw,
Y caf fynediad llon ryw dydd –
Fy Nhad sydd wrth y llyw.

On Tempestuous Seas
Evan Evans (1795–1855)

On tempestuous seas I travel
To a world where it's better to live,
While smiling at each storm it brings –
My Father's at the helm.

Through rough and perilous places,
And obstacles of every sort,
I've been dragged on my journey –
My Father's at the helm.

Despite being thrown from wave to wave,
Until I fear for my life,
I have escaped them all so far –
My Father's at the helm.

And if there's bigger storms ahead,
Reserved by my God,
I'll face them all boldly,
My Father's at the helm.

And when the swell gathers force,
My anchor is secure,
To keep me safely through them all –
My Father's at the helm.

Into the calm, safe harbour,
Away from the raging storm,
One day I'll enter happily –
My Father's at the helm

CARDIFF AND VALE COLLEGE